"Coach John Wooden's succes[s]... Coach Wooden's Greatest Secr[et]... sence of Coach Wooden's core value. Read this ... the lessons to achieve excellence in your life."

—**Mike McCarthy**, head football coach, Green Bay Packers

"*Coach Wooden's Greatest Secret* has kept me engaged from start to finish. I can't believe there is so much wisdom packed between two covers."

—**Charlie Strong**, head football coach, University of Louisville

"I am always looking for books on leadership. When I find one, it is like gold, not only for my own personal growth but for the growth of the entire organization. Pat Williams's new book on Coach Wooden will have a major impact on every reader."

—**James Franklin**, head football coach, Vanderbilt University

"In *Coach Wooden's Greatest Secret*, Pat Williams has produced a book that is a must-read for anyone who aspires to achieve excellence in any profession. The principles set forth in this book work. I can attest to that, having seen coaches Tony Dungy and Marv Levy apply them during numerous championship seasons in the NFL. In this book, Pat and Coach Wooden provide you with a blueprint for success."

—**Bill Polian**, NFL analyst for ESPN; former NFL executive

"For years we have preached that to be successful, there is nothing insignificant. There are no small things, but all things are important. Pat Williams's chronicling of Coach Wooden's philosophy and life's work vividly sets forth guidelines for a successful life."

—**Ned Colletti**, general manager, Los Angeles Dodgers

"Coach John Wooden was a man of great simplicity in every area of his life. Now, Pat Williams has captured Coach's greatest secret in this powerful little book. Don't hesitate; start reading."

—**Dom Capers**, defensive coordinator, Green Bay Packers; former head coach, Carolina Panthers and Houston Texans

"Pat Williams's latest book is a truly great read. *Coach Wooden's Greatest Secret* is filled with motivation, inspiration, and life lessons for all of us. I'll be using segments of the book with our team to further the development of the Michigan football program."

—**Brady Hoke**, head football coach, University of Michigan

"I have this book all marked up with great ideas that I can use for helping my guys. I have read almost everything that has been written about Coach Wooden, but this one really hit me right between the eyes with the message that I have been trying to preach to my players: 'Pay attention to the details in the little things, and the big things will be there.'"

—**Mike Matheny**, manager, St. Louis Cardinals

"It has been a great pleasure to read Pat's latest book, *Coach Wooden's Greatest Secret*. As a coach on any level, you will learn, gain, and reinforce pearls of wisdom that may prove to be a catalyst to empower your team or individuals. It is a very easy read and a book that you will not want to put down. There are passages I have highlighted to go back and reread on multiple occasions and to share with our coaching staff and team."

—**Marvin Lewis**, head football coach, Cincinnati Bengals

COACH WOODEN'S GREATEST SECRET

The Power of a Lot of Little Things Done Well

Pat Williams

with Jim Denney

Revell

a division of Baker Publishing Group
Grand Rapids, Michigan

© 2014 by Pat Williams

Published by Revell
a division of Baker Publishing Group
P.O. Box 6287, Grand Rapids, MI 49516-6287
www.revellbooks.com

Paperback edition published 2015
ISBN 978-0-8007-2374-3

Printed in the United States of America

The Library of Congress has cataloged the previous edition as follows:
Williams, Pat, 1940-
    Coach Wooden's greatest secret : the power of a lot of little things done well
/ Pat Williams, with Jim Denney.
        pages cm
    Includes bibliographical references.
    ISBN 978-0-8007-2276-0 (cloth)
    1. Success. 2. Change (Psychology) 3. Wooden, John, 1910-2010. I. Title.
    BJ1611.2.W463 2014
    170'.44—dc23   2013036189

15   16   17   18   19   20   21   7   6   5   4   3   2

To
our two latest grandchildren,
twin boys, Benjamin and Deacon

May the life principles of Coach Wooden's greatest secret
become a part of their lives at an early age.

<><><><><><>

"It's the little details that are vital. Little things make big things
happen."

Coach John Wooden

Contents

Foreword

I HAD THE GREAT THRILL AND HONOR OF BEING A part of two NBA championship teams, in 1999 and 2003. Yet I think the honor I received in 2004, after I retired, may have been even greater: The Keys to Life Award, personally presented to me by one of my all-time heroes, Coach John Wooden. The award is given to those who aspire to follow Coach Wooden's Seven Keys to Life:

1. Be true to yourself.
2. Help others.
3. Make each day your masterpiece.
4. Drink deeply from good books, especially the Bible.
5. Make friendship a fine art.
6. Build a shelter against a rainy day.
7. Pray for guidance and give thanks for your blessings every day.

Coach John Wooden has always been one of my role models. From observing his life and his coaching style, I learned that it is possible to be intensely competitive, to be a winner and a champion, and still be a person of integrity, humility, character, and faith. No coach ever won more championships than Coach Wooden, and no one was ever more giving and caring and unassuming than Coach Wooden.

In his entire coaching career, Coach John Wooden only had one losing season—his very first season coaching at the high school level. After that, he was all about winning. At UCLA he won 620 games in 27 seasons, had a record winning streak of 88 consecutive wins, had 4 perfect 30–0 seasons, won 98 consecutive home games at UCLA's Pauley Pavilion, and won 10 NCAA titles in 12 seasons.

Coach Wooden won when he had superstars on his team. But he also won when there were no superstars, when most of his starters had graduated and would not be returning. All of those wins and championships were not merely the result of a superstar roster. There was something special about Coach Wooden himself, about the way he coached, about the principles he taught, about the values he instilled in his players.

He had a secret formula for success. Well, it wasn't really much of a secret. If you asked him, he would readily tell you. The key to his success, he said, was a lot of little things done well. If you would focus on the little things that escaped the notice of your opponents and competitors, you would have a slight edge over them—and that would be your winning edge.

In this book, Pat Williams, the cofounder and senior vice president of the Orlando Magic, has unpacked and explored Coach John Wooden's greatest success secret so that we can all follow the example of the greatest coach of all time. In these pages, Pat examines every facet of Coach Wooden's formula for success. You'll discover how focusing on the little things will prepare you for great things. These principles will help to safeguard your character and produce habits of consistency and excellence in your life.

Success, winning, achievement, influence, leadership—these are big things. But they are the result of a lot of little things done well. Whatever your dreams and goals, whatever your field of endeavor, whatever you hope to achieve in life, this book will speed you on your journey.

David Robinson
two-time NBA world champion, San Antonio Spurs;
founder, IDEA Carver (formerly Carver Academy), San Antonio;
cofounder, Admiral Capital Group

Acknowledgments

W ITH DEEP APPRECIATION I ACKNOWLEDGE the support and guidance of the following people who helped make this book possible.

Special thanks to Alex Martins, Dan DeVos, and Rich DeVos of the Orlando Magic.

Hats off to my associate Andrew Herdliska; my proofreader, Ken Hussar; and my ace typist, Fran Thomas.

Thanks also to my writing partner, Jim Denney, for his superb contributions in shaping this manuscript.

Hearty thanks also go to Andrea Doering, senior acquisitions editor at Revell Books, and to the entire Revell team for their vision and insight and for believing that we had something important to say in these pages.

And, finally, special thanks and appreciation go to my wife, Ruth, and to my wonderful and supportive family. They are truly the backbone of my life.

Introduction

Little Things Make Big Things Happen

Big things are accomplished only through the perfection of minor details.

Coach John Wooden

IN JULY 2000, I CHECKED MY VOICE MAIL AND HEARD a message that changed my life. "Mr. Williams," the caller said, "this is John Wooden, former basketball coach at UCLA." I was amazed that the greatest coach in the history of college basketball thought he needed to explain to me who he was.

Coach Wooden went on to give his personal recommendation for a UCLA trainer who had applied for a position with the Orlando Magic. He ended the message by saying, "I enjoy reading your books very much. Good-bye."

I returned his call, and we had a wonderful chat. It was the first of many encounters I was to have with Coach John Wooden in the years to come. A few months later, as I was thinking about writing a book called *How to Be like Coach Wooden*, I wrote to him and asked for his blessing on the project. A few days later, he called and again said, "Mr. Williams, this is John Wooden, former basketball coach at UCLA."

I thought, *Coach, I truly do know who you are!*

"I received your letter," he said, "and even though I'm not worthy of a project like this, if you would like to write this book, you go right ahead."

That was the beginning of my friendship with Coach Wooden—a friendship that resulted in a series of books about his life and his philosophy. I followed *How to Be like Coach Wooden* (2006) with *Coach Wooden: The Seven Principles That Shaped His Life and Will Change Yours* (2011) and this book, *Coach Wooden's Greatest Secret*.

During the last decade of his life, Coach Wooden invited me into his life in an extraordinary way. Not only did I have many rewarding conversations with him, but I also interviewed literally hundreds of people who knew him and had great stories to tell and insights to share. As I got to know Coach Wooden, as I heard story after story about him, it occurred to me that if everyone in the world was more like him, this world would be almost problem-free.

A number of times, I went to Coach's condo in Encino, California, to pick him up and take him out to dinner. At five o'clock sharp, we'd head out to the Valley Inn, Coach Wooden's favorite dining spot, located in Sherman Oaks. We'd arrive in time for the Early Bird Special. His favorite item on the menu was the Valley Inn's famous clam chowder.

As we conversed over dinner, I was always impressed by the clarity of Coach Wooden's thinking, the depth of his wisdom, and the quickness of his gentle sense of humor. You soon forgot that you were talking to a man in his nineties, because he had the mind of a much younger man.

Mark Gottfried, a former assistant at UCLA, now the head basketball coach at North Carolina State, once told me, "Whenever you're with Coach Wooden, you'd better have a catcher's mitt on. You never know when Coach might toss you an important wisdom principle, so you'd better be ready to snag it."

I also found out, in my conversations with Coach, that it wasn't enough to be a good listener. I had to have my thinking cap on whenever I was around him. Coach was a consummate educator, teacher, and mentor. He favored the Socratic method of asking questions and challenging your answers in order to force you to think. Many times, he would pepper me with probing questions. Whether I was answering his questions or he was answering mine, it was always a profound learning experience for me.

At one of our dinners together, I was fortunate to have both my thinking cap and my catcher's mitt on. I asked him, "Coach, if you could pinpoint just one secret of success in life, what would it be?"

Coach would never give a glib or superficial answer. If you asked him a thoughtful question, he would take a few moments to think through what he wanted to say. He was constantly aware of his influence, and he always wanted to give people the very best of his wisdom. As I waited for his answer, I found myself leaning closer, anticipating his insight, not wanting to miss a single syllable.

He said, "The closest I can come to one secret of success is this: a lot of little things done well."

That was a eureka moment for me.

I have given hundreds of speeches and have written dozens of books on success and motivation. Yet, in that one magical moment, in a single seven-word phrase, Coach Wooden crystallized everything I have been trying to communicate for decades: a lot of little things done well.

The Difference between Winning and Losing

Coach John Wooden was the greatest coach who ever lived. That's not just my opinion. That's the consensus throughout the sports world.

In July 2009, the *Sporting News* published a ranking of the fifty greatest coaches of all time, in every sport, at every level, both collegiate and professional. The ranking was made by a blue-ribbon committee of sportswriters, coaches, and top athletes. The number one coach on that list was John Wooden, followed by Vince Lombardi and Bear Bryant. During his tenure as head basketball coach of the UCLA Bruins (1948–75), Coach John Wooden won ten NCAA national championships in a twelve-year period, including seven championships in a row. During that time, his Bruins won a record eighty-eight games in a row. His record is unprecedented and is likely to stand as long as the game of basketball is played.

Coach Wooden is remembered for the many inspirational talks and motivational tools he gave his players, especially his Pyramid of Success. He was also famed for never screaming, never cussing, never berating his players but always speaking calmly yet firmly. His players didn't fear his wrath, but they feared disappointing him. They loved him, and out of that love, they played their hearts out for him.

One of Coach Wooden's most famous and accomplished players was Kareem Abdul-Jabbar (known during his college days as Lew Alcindor). Kareem wrote these words of tribute to Coach Wooden in a December 2000 op-ed for the *New York Times*:

> Thirty-five years ago, I walked into John Wooden's office at UCLA and began a special relationship that has enriched my life. . . . He was soft-spoken and serious, yet his caring demeanor drew me to him. He always called me Lewis, not Lew or Lewie,

the way everyone else did back then. Today, he calls me Kareem, although sometimes he slips up and calls me Lewis.

He was more a teacher than a coach. He broke basketball down to its basic elements. He always told us basketball was a simple game, but his ability to make the game simple was part of his genius.

I never remember him yelling on the court, but there was no need because he never had trouble getting his point across. I remember a close game in my sophomore year against Colorado State. During timeouts, his instructions were clear and precise. I had never doubted him before, but when the game ended, it was obvious he had been thinking three moves ahead of us, calm and cool as always.[1]

Coach Wooden always seemed to think three moves ahead of everyone else. Whenever I was with him, I felt like I was a student and he was the master, the mentor, the teacher. And if I needed insight, I needed only to lower my bucket into the well of his wisdom, and there would always be plenty of insight to draw from.

So on that evening when he told me that the key to success in life is "a lot of little things done well," I felt I had fallen into a gold mine. Those seven words matched up exactly with everything I had experienced in my own journey toward success—and they matched up with the experiences of successful people in many fields.

Miami Heat shooting guard Dwyane Wade was named 2006 Sportsman of the Year by *Sports Illustrated*. He helped lead the Heat to two NBA championships (2006 and 2012). He also helped lead the 2008 United States men's basketball "Redeem Team" to a gold medal in the 2008 Beijing Summer Olympics. He ascribes his success to little things, saying, "Guys who might not be superstars, but because of their hustle, because of the little things they do, these are the guys who can really mean the difference between winning and losing."[2]

Swimmer Ryan Lochte, who won two Olympic gold medals in Beijing and two more gold medals in the 2012 London Summer Olympics, also says that the difference between winning and losing is the little things: "I'm going to focus on speed, doing little things like my turns and my starts—just speed."[3]

But the little things are also important in fields that have nothing to do with athletic competition. Sir Roger Penrose is an English mathematical physicist. He shared the 1988 Wolf Prize for physics with Stephen Hawking. He once explained that the discovery of a grand scientific principle often takes place not as a sudden, huge revelation but as a series of small inklings, one idea building on top of another. "People think of these eureka moments," he once said, "and my feeling is that they tend to be little things, a little realization, and then a little realization built on that."[4]

Bruce Barton was an advertising executive, the cofounder of the Batten, Barton, Durstine & Osborn (BBDO) agency. He invented Betty Crocker and named the companies General Electric and General Motors. He also served as a two-term congressman from the state of New York. Barton once observed, "Sometimes when I consider what tremendous consequences come from little things, I am tempted to think there are no little things."[5]

Samuel Johnson, the eighteenth-century English writer and literary critic, has been called "the most distinguished man of letters in English history." He understood the importance of little things to the art of living well. He once wrote, "There is nothing, Sir, too little for so little a creature as man. It is by studying little things that we attain the great art of having as little misery and as much happiness as possible."[6]

The Little Things within the Big Picture

NCAA coaching legend Dean Smith coached men's basketball for thirty-six years (1961–97) at the University of North Carolina at Chapel Hill, retiring with 879 victories to his credit. Dave Odom, who coached basketball at Wake Forest, recalls the warm-ups before a game between his Wake Forest Demon Deacons and Dean Smith's Tar Heels.

"I saw a couple of [Dean Smith's] assistants watching the team do layups and writing something down," Odom said. "I was curious and asked what they were doing. Turns out they were charting the layups. If any were missed, [Smith] addressed that in practice the next day. At first, I thought he was crazy, but then I realized that here was a man who devoted himself to every possible facet of the game." In other words, Dean Smith was focused on the little things that can make the difference between winning and losing.[7]

Charles Walgreen (1873–1939) was an American businessman and founder of the Walgreens drugstore chain. It was a little thing—part of his finger—that led to him becoming a drugstore mogul. At age sixteen, he was working in a shoe factory, operating a machine that cut leather for shoes. His hand slipped, and he cut off the top joint of one of his fingers. The doctor who treated him persuaded him to take a job as an apprentice for local pharmacist D. S. Horton. As a result of his employment, Walgreen became fascinated with the drugstore trade. By the time he was twenty-eight, he owned his own pharmacy in Chicago. Fifteen years later, he owned nine stores. Ten years after that, he owned more than one hundred.

Walgreen once wrote a book called *Set Your Sales for Bigger Earnings*, and he made sure that every sales employee of his drugstore empire received a copy. In that book, he wrote, "Success is doing a thousand little things the right way—doing many of them over and over again."[8] Like Coach John Wooden, like Dwyane Wade and Ryan Lochte, like Sir Roger Penrose and Bruce Barton and Samuel Johnson, Charles Walgreen understood the importance of a lot of little things done well.

Writing in *Fast Company*, Alan Cohen asks, "Why do some people succeed and others don't? Two sports teams with equal talent and the same records. One wins the championship and the other doesn't. Why? . . . What is the difference between being successful and being mediocre? It is taking the time to do the little things. It is that simple."[9]

Stanford business school professor and researcher Robert Sutton reports that one of the distinguishing marks of a good business leader (a "good boss") is that he or she is interested in the little things, the details of the organization. An ineffective and arrogant business leader (a "bad boss") is interested only in the big picture and considers the little things unworthy of notice. "Big picture" bosses, says Sutton, tend to "see generating big and vague ideas as the important part of their jobs—and to treat implementation, or pesky details of any kind, as mere 'management work' best done by 'the little people.' . . . [They] avoid learning about people they lead, technologies their companies use, customers they serve, and numerous other crucial little things."

Sutton cites the example of a CEO of a major cellular phone company who made a series of disastrous product development and marketing decisions because all he cared about was the big picture. This CEO was out of touch with the features consumers really wanted in their phones, the little things his customers were looking for—so the marketplace rejected his company's products.

By contrast, Sutton says, the late Apple CEO Steve Jobs was able to envision the big picture while also maintaining a focus on the little things. From the time Apple opened its first Apple Store near Jobs's home in Palo Alto, the CEO himself would often visit the store. Sutton writes, "Jobs constantly fussed over details such as the quality of the shopping bags, where employees stood in the store, and the color of the walls and tables, and what they conveyed about the brand." One of the keys to Steve Jobs's brilliance was his ability to focus on the little things within the big picture.

As Sutton concludes, "I am all for big ideas, visions, and dreams. But the best bosses do more than think big thoughts. They have a deep understanding of their industries, organizations, and teams, the people they lead, as well as other mundane things. . . . This ability to go back and forth between the little details and the big picture is evident in the leaders I admire most."[10]

Leaders can delegate tasks and authority, but leaders cannot delegate responsibility. A leader is responsible for every action and decision made by the people under his command. Great leaders build teams of creative self-starters, then empower their people to make decisions. They set clear objectives and standards, then they check in often to make sure those objectives and standards are met. By paying attention to the little things, great leaders accomplish big things.

After the end of World War I, Eastman Kodak founder George Eastman began planning a large theater for the city of Rochester, New York, where his company was headquartered. Eastman envisioned the theater as home to performances of music, dance, and silent films with orchestral accompaniment. As he examined the blueprints for the theater, which would contain more than three thousand seats, he told the architect, "We could probably add another two seats here."

When the architect expressed surprise that Eastman would concern himself with such a small detail, Eastman explained, "Let's say that each seat would bring in thirty cents per performance, or sixty cents for the two seats. With six performances, that would add up to three dollars and sixty cents per week. In a year, that might amount to one hundred eighty-seven dollars and twenty cents—which, by the way, is the interest on three thousand one hundred twenty dollars for a year."

George Eastman got his two extra seats, and the Eastman Theatre opened on September 4, 1922. That beautiful theater stands today as the performance venue for the Rochester Philharmonic Orchestra and the Eastman School of Music. Today those thirty-cent seats sell for between $22 and $79 each.[11]

Little things have a way of making a big impact over time. George Eastman clearly understood the insight that Coach Wooden shared with me one evening over steaming bowls of clam chowder: The most important secret of success in any enterprise, from sports to business to science to entertainment, is a lot of little things done well. Or, as Coach Wooden put it in his 2005 bestseller, *Wooden on Leadership*, "Little things make big things happen."

In the following chapters, we will look at the various ways we can apply Coach Wooden's most powerful success secret to all the arenas of our lives. Put on your thinking cap and your catcher's mitt as we begin our journey through Coach Wooden's greatest success secret.

Big things are about to happen in your life.

1

Little Things Are Fundamental to Achievement

I discovered early on that the player who learned the fundamentals of basketball is going to have a much better chance of succeeding and rising through the levels of competition than the player who was content to do things his own way.

Coach John Wooden

SOON AFTER I BECAME ACQUAINTED WITH COACH Wooden, I was surprised to discover that he didn't consider himself primarily a coach. He saw himself, first and foremost, as a teacher. If you asked him, "How many years did you coach?" he would always correct the premise of your question: "I was a *teacher* for forty years—eleven years in high school, twenty-nine years in college."

When Coach and I got together over a meal or chatted at his condo, we rarely talked about coaching or basketball or sports at all. We talked a lot about his faith and values, his heroes

(Abraham Lincoln and Mother Teresa), his love of poetry and literature, and his love of teaching. The great joy of his life was the opportunity he had as a teacher to impact generations of young people. Even when he was coaching basketball, most of his effort was focused not on the game but on preparing the young men on his team to be effective, productive human beings.

Often, after Coach and I shared a meal together at the Valley Inn, we'd return to his home and the light on his answering machine would be blinking. There was almost always a message from at least one of his former players. Coach had been retired for more than three decades, yet he still received calls from men who had played for him from the late 1940s to the 1970s. Some called simply to keep in touch. Some called for advice. All of them called because of what this man had meant in their lives as a teacher, mentor, and role model. Coach Wooden's players kept in touch through the years because they loved him. And they loved him because he had always loved them.

As a coach and a teacher, John Wooden focused on the little things. He was a teacher of the fundamentals. Coach Wooden once wrote a short piece for *Newsweek* explaining his approach to the fundamentals:

> I think it's the little things that really count. The first thing I would show our players at our first meeting was how to take a little extra time putting on their shoes and socks properly. The most important part of your equipment is your shoes and socks. You play on a hard floor. So you must have shoes that fit right. And you must not permit your socks to have wrinkles around the little toe—where you generally get blisters—or around the heels. . . . Once I started teaching that many years ago, it did cut down on blisters. It definitely helped. But that's just a little detail that coaches must take advantage of, because it's the little details that make the big things come about.[1]

Coach Wooden was a stickler for teaching all those little details known as the fundamentals. "In my profession," he once wrote, "fundamentals included such 'trivial' issues as insisting on double-tying of shoelaces, seeing that uniforms were properly fitted, and getting players in position to rebound every missed shot. The perfection of those little things—making a habit of doing them right—usually determines if a job is done well or done poorly. It's true for any organization."[2]

Run to Win the Prize

Jack Ramsay is a former basketball coach and the man who gave me my first job in the NBA. When he took over as coach of the Portland Trail Blazers in 1976, Dr. Jack's first order of business was to talk to his star center (and Coach Wooden protégé), Bill Walton. "I met with Bill Walton," he recalled, "to explain the game I wanted to play and his role in it. He seemed pleased with the theory, and yet I remember his comment as we finished our meeting: 'Coach, one last thing—don't assume we know anything.'"[3]

What did Walton mean by that? He was telling his new coach that he and his teammates were eager to learn the fundamentals of playing basketball at the NBA level. Even after four years of playing for Coach Wooden at UCLA, Bill Walton knew there were still *more* fundamentals to be learned and mastered at this new and more intense level of competition. When Jack Ramsay heard that Bill Walton and his teammates were eager students of the fundamentals, he knew he'd have a great team—and he was right. That season, Dr. Jack coached the Trail Blazers to an NBA championship.

Lou Holtz served as head football coach at six universities, including a decade-plus tenure at the University of Notre Dame (1986–96). He's the only coach in collegiate football to lead six different programs to bowl games, and he took four of those programs to top twenty national rankings. Business leader and motivational writer Harvey Mackay recalls an incident he witnessed that says a lot about Coach Lou Holtz's attention to the little things:

> Lou Holtz is a stickler for details. When he was the head football coach at Notre Dame, I was able to join him for a road game at Purdue. His student athletes were instructed to wear coats and ties to the stadium because they'd be closely observed as representatives of the University of Notre Dame. They were waiting to board the bus to go to the stadium for the game. And waiting. Coach Holtz showed up. Didn't say a word. Just went down the line and looked them over. And over. Finally he went up to one of the players, smiled, reached up and straightened the player's tie, and then nodded to the driver of the bus. Not until then was the door to the bus opened and the team permitted to load up.
>
> He hadn't said anything, but the message was as clear as if he had tattooed it across the center's fanny: If you're going to be a winner, guys, look like a winner. Little things mean everything.[4]

Former Major League Baseball manager Whitey Herzog has been a player, manager, general manager, scout, and farm system director. As a manager, he led the Kansas City Royals to three consecutive play-off appearances (1976 to 1978) and led the St. Louis Cardinals to three World Series appearances, including one championship. In *You're Missin' a Great Game*, Whitey observed:

> Baseball, when it's played right, is made up of a lot of smaller plays, and each one gives you an edge if you work at it. It's also a game of large samples: Over 154 or 162 games, the little things accumulate and pile up and turn into big ones. That's the game's most essential fact. It's a game of percentages, and any way you can tilt the wheel your way a little, you do. Casey [former Yankees manager Casey Stengel] tilted it one degree here, another degree

there, till the ball just seemed to roll the Yankees' way and he looked up in August and saw New York right where they always seem to be, at the top of the standings, looking down. Writers and fans hardly ever notice these little things, and you hardly ever hear anybody mention 'em, but they decide championships. No good club ever won a thing without 'em.[5]

Baseball catcher and manager Yogi Berra spent most of his playing career with the Yankees, playing under manager Casey Stengel. Yogi agrees with Whitey Herzog that Casey Stengel was a master of the little things, a fanatic about the fundamentals. In his autobiography, Yogi recalled:

Doing the little things can make a big difference. It doesn't matter whether you're working around the house or playing baseball, there is always a right way and a wrong way, and it's the little details that mean a lot. Paying attention to the basics—in baseball, it's the fundamentals—is a little thing that's a big thing.

You always hear about not sweating the small stuff. Well, some little things they say you shouldn't worry about are more important than the big stuff. It's better to never assume anything.

I was real lucky to play for Casey Stengel, who was a stickler for fundamentals, and we practiced them all the time. Casey used to say that most games are lost, not won, meaning that when you mess up the little fundamentals—making a cutoff play, advancing a runner when making an out—you're not going to win. . . .

Casey was great with young players, too, because he liked teaching them all the little stuff that was important. He actually started the instructional league (he called it the "instructural" league) to help rookies; he knew that making them know the little things would give us an advantage.[6]

These insights from Whitey Herzog and Yogi Berra apply not only in sports but in business, education, politics, and every other field of endeavor. If you master those little skills called the fundamentals, you tilt the playing field in your favor. With every new fundamental skill you acquire, you tilt it a little bit more. The difference any one fundamental skill makes in your overall performance will be minimal, almost imperceptible, but add up all those little increments over time, and they will give you a huge edge over your opponents and all the obstacles you face.

Michael Jordan's biography on the National Basketball Association's website says, "By acclamation, Michael Jordan is the greatest basketball player of all time."[7] Jordan's individual accomplishments include five MVP awards, fourteen NBA All-Star Game appearances, six NBA Finals MVP awards, and being named the greatest North American athlete of the twentieth century by ESPN. He credits his accomplishments to coaches who taught him early in life to master the fundamentals. "When I was young," he once said, "I had to learn the fundamentals of basketball. You can have all the physical ability in the world, but you still have to know the fundamentals."[8]

Tony Dungy has two NFL Championship rings, one as a Pittsburgh Steelers cornerback in Super Bowl XIII, one as head coach of the Indianapolis Colts in Super Bowl XLI (the Colts made the play-offs in every season of Dungy's tenure). He retired from coaching in 2009 and is currently the spokesman for All Pro Dad, a national fatherhood program.

In September 2010, Coach Dungy was invited to speak to the New York Yankees before a game against the Red Sox. Reporters asked Coach Dungy what he told the Yankees. He replied, "We talked about some of our experiences, focusing, hanging together down the stretch, important games. It's not necessarily who has the most talent but what team sticks together and executes their fundamentals the best. Probably nothing they haven't heard from [Yankees manager] Joe [Girardi]. But I know I have a son who doesn't listen to anything I say and if he hears the same thing from someone else, sometimes it has a little more impact."

It's true. Down deep, we all know that success demands that we master and execute the fundamentals—the little things that give us a big edge against tough competition. Like Coach Dungy's son, many of us need to hear it again, from a different person, from a different perspective, from a different direction, before it really sinks in.[9]

Entrepreneur and motivational writer-speaker Jim Rohn has influenced millions and has mentored such master motivators as Brian Tracy and *Chicken Soup for the Soul* authors Mark Victor Hansen and Jack Canfield. Jim Rohn once said, "Success is neither magical nor mysterious. Success is the natural consequence of consistently applying the basic fundamentals."[10]

The importance of mastering and applying the fundamentals is truly ancient wisdom. In Bible times, the apostle Paul wrote, "Do you not know that in a race all the runners run, but only one gets the prize? Run in such a way as to get the prize. Everyone who competes in the games goes into strict training. They do it to get a crown that will not last, but we do it to get a crown that will last forever. Therefore I do not run like someone running aimlessly; I do not fight like a boxer beating the air. No, I strike a blow to my body and make it my slave so that after I have preached to others, I myself will not be disqualified for the prize" (1 Cor. 9:24–27).

Most of what Paul says in those verses has to do with self-discipline, yet if you read carefully, you see that Paul is also talking about applying the fundamentals. It does no good to spend hours and hours training in the wrong techniques and building bad habits. If you want to win the prize, you must master the fundamentals. You have to avoid bad habits such as overstriding (leg movement too far forward) and overkicking (leg movement too far behind). You have to avoid clenching your fists or tensing your face. You need to keep your trunk at just the right angle. You must maintain a vertical head position. These are just a few of the many fundamentals a successful runner must learn. If a runner doesn't master the fundamentals, Paul says, he'll run aimlessly, like a boxer beating the air.

So take the advice of Coach Wooden, Coach Holtz, Coach Herzog, Coach Jordan, Coach Dungy, Coach Rohn, and Coach Paul. To win the prize, master the fundamentals and apply them every day.

Turn a Big Challenge into a Lot of Little Things

It's easy to see how a master-the-fundamentals approach can make a big difference in athletics and sports. But can we apply the same principle to other areas of life? Absolutely!

Former New York City mayor Rudy Giuliani dramatically reduced the crime rate in that city by applying the fundamentals. When he came into office, crime was out of control. A survey of residents showed that more than half of New Yorkers said they would move out if they could afford to. New York had acquired a reputation as a dirty, dangerous, depressing city. Giuliani had his work cut out for him. Former US attorney general John Ashcroft describes how Giuliani transformed the social environment in New York:

> Giuliani started by going after the little things. "I am a firm believer in the theory that 'minor' crimes and 'quality of life' offenses are all part of the larger picture," he explains. Among the first elements to go were the "Squeegee Men," drug-addicted and shady-looking riffraff who personified New York's rough edge. Armed with a soiled rag and a dirty bottle of watered-down Windex, these men would bully and badger motorists for money.
>
> Giuliani said, "We are not going to put up with this anymore," and he brought this intimidation to an end. He then declared war on graffiti, subway panhandlers, loitering, broken windows, and petty vandalism—minor offenses that would have gone

unnoticed in days past while the police force was overwhelmed with homicides and violent crime. . . .

[Giuliani explained,] "Small problems can be the first step to big trouble. Neighborhoods scarred by graffiti or blasted day and night by boom-box radios will become besieged, vulnerable, and ultimately dangerous places. If police departments surrender on the small issues—using the excuse that they are too busy dealing with 'serious' crime—they soon find themselves surrendering to the latter as well."[11]

Mayor Giuliani achieved big results by focusing on the little things, by paying attention to the fundamentals of a decent and law-abiding society. From 1993 to 1996, the murder rate plummeted by nearly 50 percent. Robberies dropped by 42 percent, and auto thefts dropped by 46 percent. During the previous mayor's administration, no one dared to imagine such results were possible. The streets and sidewalks of New York became safe and inviting once more because Mayor Giuliani came in with a brand-new focus-on-the-fundamentals approach.[12]

The same principles apply to the world of business. As Stanford business professor Robert Sutton observes, about eleven thousand new business books are published each year by "armies of consultants, gurus, and wannabe thought leaders." They all claim that their ideas are new and improved and that business, management, and leadership principles need to be "reinvented." While acknowledging that such factors as globalization and the internet have impacted the business world in new ways, Sutton notes that every generation has faced change—for example, the introduction of the locomotive, the telegraph, the telephone, and air travel.

Yet in spite of all these changes, Sutton writes, "the fundamentals of what it takes to lead, organize, and inspire followers were pretty much 'the same as it ever was.' . . . We humans still yearn to follow others who are competent enough to bring in resources, teach us new skills, and . . . make us feel cared for and respected. . . . The fundamentals remain unchanged."[13]

I agree. The fundamentals of leadership, whether in sports or business or the military or the church, are the same now as they have always been. I call the fundamentals of leadership "The Seven Sides of Leadership." They are:

1. *Vision.* Successful leaders are visionaries who dream of a brighter future, then lead people toward the fulfillment of that vision.
2. *Communication skills.* Successful leaders are skilled communicators who are able to convey their vision and energize their people.
3. *People skills.* Successful leaders know how to make people feel respected, empowered, and valued.
4. *Character.* Successful leaders are people of integrity, courage, hard work, fairness, and good judgment. Their good character inspires people to follow them.
5. *Competence.* Successful leaders have the experience and the ability to make their teams and organizations competitive.
6. *Boldness.* Successful leaders are decisive and courageous. Their boldness inspires confidence in their people.
7. A *serving heart.* Successful leaders are not bosses; they are servants of the people they lead.

These are the seven fundamentals of leadership. No one is born with all these traits, but they are all learnable skills—if we will be teachable leaders. Successful leaders are attentive to the fundamentals of leadership.

Many people dream of owning their own business—yet they fail to take the time to learn the fundamentals of operating a successful business. The fundamentals are not difficult to learn— that's why they're called fundamentals. Though the fundamentals are simple to understand, the daily chore of applying those fundamentals takes commitment, effort, and self-discipline.

One of the fundamentals of business is *planning*—making sure you have enough start-up capital, making sure you track sales and control expenses, and making sure you market your business effectively to the public. Another fundamental is *people*—finding the right people for the right jobs and knowing how to manage them well. Another fundamental is *processes*— the actions you and your employees carry out every day to ensure consistent, high-quality products or services. To be successful in business, you have to be attentive to all the little things, all the fundamentals of running a successful business. If you lose track of the fundamentals, the dream quickly becomes a nightmare.

When a business fails, it's usually because the boss lost track of the fundamentals. When students fail, it's usually because they neglected to learn the fundamentals and therefore lacked a fundamental knowledge base to build on. When wars are lost, the defeat can often be traced to a disastrous failure by military commanders to apply the fundamentals.

The Korean War erupted five years after the end of World War II. When Lieutenant General Walton H. Walker, commander of the Eighth Army, was killed in a jeep crash, World War II hero General Matthew Ridgway took over. Upon assuming command, Ridgway was horrified to find the Eighth Army in complete disarray and in full retreat from communist Chinese forces. Ridgway toured the front and talked to the infantrymen. He found the soldiers to be completely demoralized. Many endured the cold Korean winter clad in thin summer uniforms, facing shortages of food, ammunition, and other supplies while their well-fed divisional commanders lived comfortably away from the front. Ridgway moved quickly to discipline lazy officers, promote responsible ones to replace them, and order divisional and corps commanders to move onto the battlefield alongside their troops.

Ridgway discovered that Eighth Army intelligence had no idea of the location and strength of enemy forces because the army was violating fundamental rules of engagement. Instead of pursuing the enemy into the hills, the army stuck to the roads. The army failed to take prisoners to interrogate them about enemy positions. Some officers made excuses, saying their radios wouldn't work in the mountainous terrain. Ridgway had no patience with excuses. He told the officers that it was army tradition to be inventive and to do whatever it takes. If radios don't work, then send out runners or send up smoke signals—but find a way to get the job done.

In a scathing report, Ridgway told the Pentagon that, on his arrival, he had found the Eighth Army to be lacking "knowledge of infantry fundamentals" and in dire need of an "aggressive fighting spirit." But he quickly turned that situation around. He revived an old army slogan to remind his forces of the fundamentals of warfare: "Find 'em! Fix 'em! Fight 'em! Finish 'em!" By returning the Eighth Army to a focus on the fundamentals, Ridgway restored morale, cohesion, and unit loyalty in his men. He took a defeated and demoralized army and within a few short weeks completely transformed it into a dominant fighting force. Under his leadership, the Eighth Army launched a counteroffensive that sent Chinese forces reeling in retreat.[14]

In April 1951, when President Truman removed General Mac-Arthur as commander of American forces in the Far East, he replaced him with General Matthew Ridgway—the leader whose focus on the fundamentals had saved South Korea from being overrun. What's true in sports, in business, and in war is equally true in every other aspect of life. If we are faithful in the little things, if we master and apply the fundamentals, we will rarely be beaten by the big things.

"At High Speed and without Conscious Thought"

One of the great advantages of maintaining a focus on the fundamentals is that it enables us to break down big challenges and problems into bite-sized pieces. When we face a huge, towering, lofty goal, it's easy to be intimidated and paralyzed with fear. But if we tell ourselves, "Let's break down this goal into its fundamental components; let's turn this big thing into a lot of little things," it suddenly becomes manageable. Our fear evaporates. We feel confident because reaching the goal is simply a matter of mastering and applying the fundamentals. What is the looming challenge in your life that has you paralyzed with fear and self-doubt? Simply apply the fundamentals, cut that challenge down to size, conquer it, and move on.

This approach to teaching is known as the "whole-part" or "whole-part-whole" approach. Professor Steve Turley of California State University, Long Beach, explains that Coach Wooden's "basic teaching theory was whole-part-whole: introduce the big concept, break it down into its constituent parts, then reconstruct the whole with a new awareness of its meaning and use. . . . Wooden's method included three pedagogical 'laws': explanation/demonstration, imitation/correction, and repetition."[15] *Sports Illustrated*'s Alexander Wolff similarly observed that Coach Wooden taught by breaking every concept down into its fundamentals:

> Wooden taught by using the "whole-part" method, breaking the game down to its elements—"just like parsing a sentence," he would say, sounding like the English teacher he had indeed once been. He applied the four basic laws of learning: explanation, demonstration, correction, and repetition. And he developed a pedagogy resting on the notion that basketball is a game of threes: forward, center, guard; shoot, drive, pass; ball, you, man; conditioning, skill, teamwork.

As a coach who shunned recruiting, put relatively little stock in the scouting of opponents, and refused to equate success with winning, Wooden figured to have become a great failure rather than college sports' preeminent winner of all time. An article of faith among coaches holds that one must be intolerant of mistakes, but here, too, Wooden was a contrarian. He considered errors to be precious opportunities for teaching—preferably in practice, of course. And the games were exams.[16]

Author and retired basketball coach Myron Finkbeiner remembers watching Coach Wooden drilling his UCLA Bruins during the Final Four in 1975. "It was amazing to watch them," Finkbeiner told me, "because Coach put them through the same drills he had used on the first day of practice at the beginning of the season. They ran through simple little passing drills, pivoting moves, blocking out routines. John Wooden was redoing the fundamentals all over again."

Pete Blackman, who played for Coach Wooden from 1958 to 1962, recited to me some unforgettable wisdom he learned from Coach Wooden: "Do the basics right and do as well as you can with what God gave you, and you will be surprised at how far you can get in life."

Coach Wooden's single-minded focus on the fundamentals goes back to the earliest days of his teaching and coaching career at South Bend Central High School in Indiana. While in South Bend, he had an experience that transformed the way he coached basketball practices. Coach Wooden befriended Notre Dame football coach Frank Leahy, and Leahy invited him to visit a Notre Dame football practice. Coach Wooden saw how the Notre Dame players moved rapidly from drill to drill whenever Leahy blew his whistle. Practices were not long, but they were fast paced, well organized, and amazingly effective. Years later, Coach Wooden recalled:

Organization became a primary asset of my coaching method-
ology—the ability to use time with great efficiency. Practices
were taut and fast-moving. I was able to accomplish this with
three-by-five cards and the meticulous advance planning that
went into what was written on them. . . .

There wasn't one second in the whole practice when anybody
was standing around wondering what would come next. . . .
The whole thing was synchronized; each hour offered up sixty
minutes, and I squeezed every second out of every minute.

Players felt, at times, that the actual game against an opponent was slower than our practice in the gym. That's exactly
the way I designed it.[17]

Coach Wooden's goal was to instill the fundamentals into his
players in such a way that they would execute them with precision, automatically and unconsciously—and unhesitatingly. He
once authored a book explaining how he schooled his players
in the fundamentals of basketball. He wrote:

It is the cumulative effect of doing a lot of little things correctly
that eventually makes a big difference in competition. . . . [What]
is the difference between the winners and losers? What caused
that errant pass, missed shot, or fumbled ball? The answer is
found in the areas of fundamentals and attention to detail.

Without the ability of all players to quickly and properly execute the fundamentals of basketball at high speed and without
conscious thought, following the principles of effective offense
won't make much difference. All of these principles are dependent
on quick, timely, and accurate passing; aggressive receiving; sharp
cutting; proper pivoting; skilled dribbling; and quick shooting (with
passing and receiving being the two most important fundamentals).
Any coach who does not understand that his primary responsibility
is to create fundamentally sound players doesn't get it.[18]

Whatever challenge we face, whatever goal we strive for,
whatever dream or vision we reach for, it can be broken down

into a set of fundamentals. Mastering those fundamentals is a key ingredient of Coach Wooden's "secret sauce" for success. Here are some handy principles to remember about mastering and applying the fundamentals:

- *The fundamentals are the little things that make a big difference.* Knowing how to put on your shoes and socks is a little thing, a fundamental thing, so basic few people give it any thought—but Coach Wooden not only thought about it but also taught his players this fundamental skill. Did it make a difference? Would you tell a coach with ten NCAA national championships he was wasting his time?

- *If you are a leader, always assume the people you lead should relearn the fundamentals.* As Bill Walton said to Dr. Jack Ramsay, "Don't assume we know anything."

- *Always be teachable.* If a mentor, instructor, coach, or leader wants to teach you the fundamentals, be a willing and eager learner. Keep an open mind. Be humble enough to learn all over again how to put on your shoes and socks.

- *Don't try to absorb everything at once.* Learn one of the fundamentals, master it, then learn the next one, and the next one, and the next one—then put them all together. Whether in sports, business, the military, the church, or any other field, the fundamentals of your trade are learnable skills. Every time you add a new skill to your arsenal, you tilt the playing field a little more in your favor.

- *Break problems down into the fundamentals.* One of the most effective ways to tackle any big problem is to follow the example of Coach Wooden and Mayor Giuliani: start at the level of the fundamentals. Start by solving the smaller, simpler problems first. Attack the root causes of the problem. Break the problem down into bite-sized chunks instead of trying to digest it all at once.

- *Focus on mastery.* Before taking on a big, new challenge— starting a new business, pursuing a degree in higher education, running for political office, or writing a book—take time to study and master the fundamentals. When people fail at a new challenge, it's often because they went in with ignorant overconfidence and not enough respect for the fundamentals.

- *Drill until the fundamentals become instinctive.* Whether you are teaching or learning the fundamentals, make sure you spend adequate time in practice. Remember how Coach Wooden learned to run a fast-paced, well-disciplined practice from football coach Frank Leahy? Whatever fundamentals you need to learn, learn them so well that you can execute them automatically, with precision, without having to think or hesitate. The goal of practicing and drilling the fundamentals is to transform a learned skill into an instinctive habit.

As Coach Wooden himself said, "The greatest holiday feast is eaten one bite at a time. Gulp it down all at once and you get indigestion. I discovered the same is true in teaching. To be effective, a leader must dispense information in bite-size digestible amounts."[19] Coach Wooden's goal should be your goal and mine: learn the fundamentals, master the fundamentals, teach the fundamentals to others, and apply the fundamentals in every area of our lives. Mastering the fundamentals is one of a lot of little things done well that make a big difference in our pursuit of success.

2

Little Things Lead to Simplicity—and Success

What I taught was as simple as one, two, three. But, without being self-congratulatory, I believe I taught "one, two, three," fairly well.

Coach John Wooden

DURING ONE VISIT TO COACH WOODEN'S HOME, I noticed an embroidered pillow on the sofa in his den. This quotation was stitched onto the pillow: "'We can do no great things, only small things with great love.' Mother Teresa." I wrote down that quotation, and I have thought about those words many times since.

Mother Teresa was a simple woman with a simple passion for helping others. She often said, "Live simply so others may simply live." Coach Wooden was profoundly impacted by the simplicity of her love for others and by the life-changing power of her focus on doing "small things with great love." He seemed to intuitively recognize that simplicity was a key to effectiveness in every endeavor, from teaching to playing the game of basketball to ministering to the poor and sick. Those who have the wisdom to "keep it simple" and who focus on the little things are the ones who accomplish great things for others and for God.

Bill Walton recalls how Coach taught the game of basketball one simple precept at a time. "Coach Wooden broke it down," Walton said, "so the players could master the fundamentals and therefore could play up to their full potential. That's the thing I remember most about UCLA basketball. The practices were more important to me than the games. The games were like an exam. . . . Every aspect of the game was broken down. . . . I remember those simple fundamentals, about getting inside yourself, looking in the mirror and making sure that you did everything that you're supposed to do, and everything else would take care of itself."[1]

If you focus on keeping it simple, don't be surprised if you are criticized for it. During Coach Wooden's heyday, sportswriters and rival coaches often derided Bruins basketball teams as "simplistic" or "predictable." They criticized Coach Wooden's game plans because they never contained any big surprises, never caught opponents off guard. All his game plans did was produce victories. His opponents always knew exactly what Coach Wooden's teams would do—but they were powerless to stop them.

Whenever sportswriters asked Coach Wooden about such criticism, he simply replied, "I'm not a strategy coach. I'm a practice coach." He once told an interviewer, "Our UCLA teams . . . kept it simple. Our opponents always said we were easy to scout but difficult to play because we executed well. . . . We weren't complicated."[2]

Of course, the best answer to his critics was his winning percentage and the championship banners that hung from the rafters of UCLA's Pauley Pavilion. Jim Harrick, who coached basketball at UCLA from 1988 to 1996, told me, "John Wooden has been described as one of the greatest teachers who ever lived. His subject was basketball and the court his classroom. He emphasized that basketball is a very simple game."

Former Bruins forward Lynn Shackelford reflects, "I get questioned about Coach Wooden every day. People ask what made him special. My answer is he kept things simple. He didn't complicate it. Basketball is a simple game. It's not meant to be complicated. It's a game of reaction. By the time you think, the guy has gone by you."[3]

Coach Wooden was a teacher who used the game of basketball to teach the game of life. He taught the most profound life principles through the simplest of means: short, memorable statements that have come to be known as maxims or "Woodenisms." Here are a few of his simple expressions of thought-provoking wisdom:

- Don't measure yourself by what you have accomplished but by what you should have accomplished with your ability.
- Ability may get you to the top, but it takes character to keep you there.
- Discipline yourself and others won't need to.
- Don't let making a living prevent you from making a life.
- You can't live a perfect day without doing something for someone who will never be able to repay you.
- Consider the rights of others before your own feelings and the feelings of others before your own rights.
- You can't let praise or criticism get to you. It's a weakness to get caught up in either one.
- Ability is a poor man's wealth.
- Never make excuses. Your friends don't need them and your foes won't believe them.
- The time to make friends is before you need them.

Ask any of Coach Wooden's most successful players—Bill Walton, Kareem Abdul-Jabbar, Jamaal Wilkes, Keith Erickson, Sidney Wicks, Gail Goodrich, and the rest—and they will tell you that they still remember Coach Wooden's maxims to this day and that they give a lot of credit for their success in life to these simple formulations of important truth. Focusing on the little things is the key to simplicity, and simplicity is one of the keys to success in basketball and in life.

Great Leaders Are Great Simplifiers

History shows that simplicity is the key to victory on the battlefield. In *This Mighty Scourge*, historian James McPherson credits the simple, uncomplicated strategic thinking of General Ulysses S. Grant for his battlefield prowess and firm decisiveness in pressure situations:

> It is one thing to describe Grant's calmness under pressure, his ability to size up a situation quickly, and his decisiveness in action. It is quite another to explain the inner sources of these strengths. Ultimately, as Sherman noted, the explanation must remain a mystery. But some things are clear. Grant possessed that most uncommon quality, common sense. He had the capacity—like Harry Truman, whom Grant resembled in many ways—to make a decision and stick with it. Union general John Schofield noted that the most extraordinary quality of Grant's "extraordinary character" was "its extreme simplicity—so extreme that many have entirely overlooked it in their search for some deeply hidden secret to account for so great a character, unmindful that simplicity is one of the most prominent attributes of greatness." Grant made it look easy.[4]

This is not merely the assessment of a historian. General Grant himself professed the conviction that simplicity is the best policy on the battlefield. During the Civil War, at the beginning of the Tennessee River Campaign in early 1862, Grant told a brigadier surgeon on his staff, "The art of war is simple enough. Find out where your enemy is. Get at him as soon as you can. Strike him as hard as you can, and keep moving on."[5] The great World War II strategist General George Patton agreed with Grant, saying, "Success in war depends upon the golden rule of war. Speed—Simplicity—Boldness."

In *Victory! Applying the Proven Principles of Military Strategy to Achieve Greater Success in Your Business and Personal Life*, motivational author Brian Tracy tells the story of a military disaster in World War II that resulted from a failure to keep it simple. That disaster is known as Operation Market Garden.

In September 1944, Field Marshal Montgomery of Great Britain prevailed upon the Allied commander, General Dwight Eisenhower, to implement his plan to bring World War II to a rapid conclusion. The plan involved seizing five strategic bridges that would enable a large and overwhelming Allied force to cross the Rhine River into Germany. While the bridges were being seized, airborne troops would parachute into enemy territory and Allied mechanized infantry would punch through the front line. It would be a massive and complex undertaking, requiring a high degree of coordination among widely separated forces.

Eisenhower initially rejected the plan because of its complexity. But Winston Churchill, who had great confidence in Field Marshal Montgomery, pressured Eisenhower to implement Operation Market Garden. Against his better judgment, Eisenhower agreed. During the planning phase, a British intelligence officer, Lieutenant-General Sir Frederick "Boy" Browning, expressed reservations about the plan, saying that in attempting to seize five bridges in a row, the Allied forces were perhaps going "a bridge too far."

The warning of Lieutenant-General Browning and the misgivings of General Eisenhower proved all too true. As the complex offensive began, thousands of paratroopers landed in the Netherlands. Because of faulty maps and bad intelligence, many were dropped far from their intended targets and were quickly surrounded by hostile forces. Communication was spotty, and the resupply of matériel and ammunition was choked off by the enemy. The Allies lost the element of surprise—which had been key to early victory—and the Germans quickly organized a massive counterattack. Thousands of Allied troops were killed or captured, and it soon became clear that Operation Market Garden had produced a humiliating and catastrophic defeat.

Witnessing the waste of so many lives on such a complex gambit was a bitter pill for General Eisenhower to swallow. More than a year before Operation Market Garden was launched, he had expressed concern that Allied forces were losing sight of one of the most important of all military principles: keep it simple. In a letter to General Thomas Handy in 1943, Eisenhower wrote, "As much as we preach simplicity in the Army, I sometimes feel it is the one thing we most frequently violated in our own thinking."[6]

Reflecting on the lessons of the Operation Market Garden fiasco, Brian Tracy writes, "The entire offensive violated the principle of simplicity from the first moment. The operation was ill conceived from the start. There were simply far too many variables, all of which had to come together at once to assure success. The complexity of the operation was such that virtually no one, at any level of command, had a clear idea of what was happening, or what could be done to minimize losses or achieve victory. In retrospect, it was a foolish waste of precious human and matériel resources."[7]

Why is simplicity so important to military strategy? Common sense tells us that in any military operation, one of the primary goals should be to confuse the enemy. But the more complicated the plan, the greater the danger that we will only confuse ourselves. Why inflict complexity and confusion on ourselves and hand that advantage over to the enemy? It makes no sense. In order to eliminate misunderstanding, confusion, and the inevitable breakdowns that multiply in complex situations, we must keep it simple. This is an essential success principle whether we are competing on the battlefield, on the basketball court, or in the business world.

In *Corps Business: The 30 Management Principles of the U.S. Marines*, business writer David Freedman makes a similar observation:

> One of the Marines' greatest tools is supposed to be: taking complex, confusing, or ambiguous situations and concepts and boiling them down to their essence. . . . [The] key to an essence is that it portrays a situation or order in a way that is easily grasped and actionable. A simple example—when a Marine commander orders that communications be established, the unit doesn't have to wonder about what sort of communications the commander has in mind. To a Marine, "establishing communications" is shorthand for "getting in touch with those units that can support us on our mission, or that we can support." Any other communications can wait.[8]

One of the best ways to keep it simple in business or on the battlefield is to avoid making policies, rules, and commands that are overly specific and complicated. Set broad goals and objectives, then empower subordinates to use their own judgment, insight, and skills in deciding how to meet those goals and objectives. In other words, give your subordinates on the front lines the authority to make on-the-spot decisions about the little things. You cannot possibly know all the operational details your people on the front lines will be aware of. So keep your own planning and decision-making processes as simple as possible and give your trusted subordinates the power to manage the little details and solve the frontline problems.

This doesn't mean you should be disengaged, of course. Make sure your subordinates report back to you on what they are doing. Hold them accountable for the results. Even though you are delegating authority, you cannot delegate responsibility. Any mistakes or failures on your watch are your responsibility. But if you recruit and train your people well, then entrust to them the authority to do their jobs, you will probably have many victories to celebrate.

David Freedman illustrates this principle with the story of Major General Emil "Buck" Bedard, who led a force of Marines into Somalia in 1992. He was sent with orders to "restore normalcy to the cities" of Somalia. Freedman writes, "The orders did not elaborate on what 'normalcy' might entail. 'I asked, "What's normal about U.S. cities?"' recalls Bedard. 'Then we decided: normalcy means people are in their homes, there isn't much violence in the streets, the kids are in school, and commerce is taking place.' This description of normalcy then became the essence of the order."[9]

In other words, Bedard's superiors gave him a broad objective and allowed him to fill in the details as he saw fit. They trusted Bedard to use good judgment in interpreting and implementing his orders. So he moved a force of nearly fifteen hundred Marines into the hinterland of Somalia. He met with the Somali tribal chiefs and told them, "We're here to help you, not harm you. I want you to form a council that is representative of your people. If you harm any of my Marines, we will kill you."[10]

With that simple message, he got the cooperation of the Somali leaders, and he set up an effective food distribution effort. Though conditions deteriorated in Somalia the following year, after General Bedard left, he proved that a keep-it-simple approach, with broad objectives that could be flexibly interpreted according to conditions on the ground, could produce excellent results, even in a chaotic African civil war.

As General Colin Powell once said, "Great leaders are almost always great simplifiers, who can cut through argument, debate and doubt, to offer a solution everybody can understand."[11]

A Strategy of Simplicity

In July 2009, when the *Sporting News* published its list of the fifty greatest coaches of all time and ranked Coach John Wooden at number one, the number two coach on the list was the late, great Vince Lombardi. Best known as the head coach of the Green Bay Packers during the 1960s, he coached the team to five NFL championships in seven years, including three in a row. Under his leadership, the Packers won the first two Super Bowl games (after the 1966 and 1967 NFL seasons).

Coach Lombardi was famed as a great motivator who could lift his teams to victory by the sheer power of his oratory. His players both feared and loved him. One of the keys to his effectiveness as a coach was his genius for simplicity. Lombardi began the first day of every training camp with a team meeting. He would stand in front of a room full of football players, hold up a football, and say, "Gentlemen, this is a football." He would talk about the football and describe its function as if his players had never seen a football before. After that, he would take his team out and show them the field, taking care to point out the yard lines, out-of-bounds lines, and end zones. Then he would inform his players that the object of the game was to take the football and move it from one end of the field to the other and get it into the end zone.

Vince Lombardi had the gift of taking a complex game involving many roles, assignments, rules, and penalties and distilling it to its essence. His son, Vince Lombardi Jr., explained:

> My father's approach to football was quite simple. His playbook was smaller than those of most other coaches, and he asked his

players to remember less than other coaches did. Simplicity—combined with discipline—was a hallmark of his method. He often said that the perfect name for the perfect football coach would be "Simple Simon Legree." This was a tongue-in-cheek comment, of course, but he liked the combination of simplicity and slave-driving implied in this fusion of personalities.[12]

Coach Lombardi believed that his players performed best when there was less to remember, less to think about, and most of what was required of them was a matter of habit and instinct. He believed that when talented teams performed poorly, the problem was usually one of overcomplication. He said, "Almost always, the plan is too complex. Too much to learn and perfect in too little time."[13]

Historian and scholar Stephen Fox described Coach Lombardi's approach to football as a masterpiece of simplicity:

> The teacher kept the lessons uncomplicated and easy to learn. "Some people try to find things in this game that don't exist," Lombardi often said. "Football is two things. It's blocking and tackling." They practiced the same few plays hundreds of times until every detail became automatic, unthinking, with every man assigned a role and responsible for it. . . . They sacrificed surprises for consistency, aiming for a modest workmanlike ideal of predictable performance and thus few mistakes. The Packers could go an entire season with only one or two botched plays. Opponents knew the sweep was coming, jabbered warnings to each other, but could not stop it. . . . The coach, team, and style of play boiled down to two qualities: discipline and simplicity. "I have been called a tyrant, but I have also been called the coach of the simplest system in football," Lombardi bantered.[14]

Leadership writer John Maxwell explains yet another facet of Coach Lombardi's simplified approach to coaching football. Maxwell writes that, at a coach's conference, "Lombardi was asked about his offensive and defensive strategies for winning football games. Other coaches had just described their elaborate schemes. Lombardi . . . responded, 'I only have two strategies. My offensive strategy is simple: When we have the ball, we aim to knock the other team down! My defensive strategy is similar: When the other team has the ball, we aim to knock all of them down!' That may sound too simple, but it really is the bottom line for winning games in the NFL."[15]

And it's the bottom line for success in any other endeavor: keep it simple. Distill everything to its essence. Drill and practice and rehearse the little things, the simple skills and habits, until they become automatic and instinctive. Then carry out your simple strategy until you win the prize.

The Art of Simplicity

Simplicity is a virtue in the arts. As painter Hans Hofmann explains, "The ability to simplify means to eliminate the unnecessary so that the necessary may speak."[16] And composer Frédéric Chopin said, "Simplicity is the final achievement. After one has played a vast quantity of notes and more notes, it is simplicity that emerges as the crowning reward of art."[17] In the early days of Apple Computer and the Apple II personal computer (circa 1977), the company's slogan was "Simplicity is the ultimate sophistication."

If simplicity is a virtue in the arts, it is even more important in the art of communication. Veteran sportscaster Dick Enberg once shared with me the lesson he learned just before his first broadcast for the Los Angeles Angels. "I was up in the booth, and I was all excited and eager to get started. Angels general manager Fred Haney came into the booth and told me, 'Let me give you the key to baseball announcing: report the ball. If you follow the ball, it will always lead to the action.' That's simple advice, but I've never forgotten it."

On April 15, 2013, the 117th running of the Boston Marathon was disrupted by terrorist explosions that killed 3 people and injured at least 183 people. The next day, McClatchy newspapers ran a story stating that the federal Department of Homeland Security had questioned the security plans of the state of Massachusetts. The story quoted the "top safety official in Massachusetts" as offering this response to the federal auditors:

> It is our hope that by conducting this and other state audits, the DHS (Office of Inspector General) gains an in-depth understanding of the realities of implementing this highly regulated and complex grant program, which differs from many other federal grant programs in that it entails initiating entirely new operating methodologies and programs; buying, installing and effectively utilizing sophisticated equipment and infrastructure; and continuously coordinating with a wide range of stakeholders to achieve myriad programmatic outcomes.[18]

Now, do you know what the top safety official in Massachusetts just said? Of course not. Nobody knows. It's what is commonly known as a "word salad." It's one long sentence written in bureaucratese, loaded with jargon, deliberately intended to be vague and obscure. Bureaucrat-speak is designed to hide the truth behind a blizzard of baffling verbiage.

If this is the way you write and speak, *stop it right now!* Learn to communicate simply and clearly. Leadership expert Sheila Murray Bethel explains:

> We use simple yet powerful language in our personal lives when we say things like "I won!" "It's a boy!" "We did it!" and "Play ball!" Let's be sure we also do so as leaders.
>
> The art of simplicity doesn't mean speaking in one-syllable words, or disavowing the language of new technology, or forsaking sensitive, eloquent language. Simplicity means not purposely complicating how you communicate. If you're going

to influence others, you need to be honest and clear in your speech. . . .

It doesn't take volumes to make an impact on people's lives. The Declaration of Independence has only 1,322 words. Lincoln's Gettysburg Address has 268, and the Lord's Prayer has 56 words. The leader who understands the art and genius of simple language has a rare gift.

The great Supreme Court Justice Oliver Wendell Holmes was invited to give an after-dinner speech. His host gave him the following advice: "What we like is to gather, gobble, gabble, and git—in that order and about that fast." As leaders, we would be wise to get on with it also. Get to the point and then "git."[19]

Leaders need to be simplifiers, especially as communicators. After Ronald Reagan was elected governor of California, he said in his inauguration address, January 5, 1967, "For many years now, you and I have been shushed like children and told there are no simple answers to the complex problems which are beyond our comprehension. Well, the truth is, there are simple answers; they just are not easy ones."

It's true. "Simple" doesn't always mean "easy." Most of the problems we face as individuals or as a society have simple solutions. We pretend that the problems are too complex to solve, but they are not really complex at all. We simply don't want to make the changes and sacrifices needed to solve them.

For example, as I write these words, the national debt grows at a rate of $4 billion per day, $170 million per hour, $2.8 million per minute, or more than $47,000 per second. That's a problem, and our leaders are failing to solve it. Why? Is the problem too complicated? No. It's astonishingly simple. All the government needs to do is what any responsible household would do if it was spending more than it was taking in: spend less. Now, spending less and balancing the budget won't be easy. But the solution really is simple. And the sooner our leaders begin to acknowledge that simple fact and begin simplifying the problem to its essence, the sooner we will get our fiscal house in order.

Great communicators are great simplifiers. Insecure people use big words and technical jargon to make themselves seem smarter or more important. Great wisdom lies in being secure enough and confident enough to communicate in simple terms, not to impress but to be clear and to be understood.

A story is told of Calvin Coolidge, a few years before he became the thirtieth president of the United States. A woman seated next to Coolidge at a banquet asked him what he did for a living.

"I am the lieutenant governor of Massachusetts," Coolidge said.

"You must tell me all about it," the woman said.

Coolidge replied, "I just did."

Take a lesson from Calvin Coolidge. Whenever you engage in the art of communication, remember that simplicity is a virtue.

"This Isn't Rocket Science"

Suze Orman is a financial adviser, author, and motivational speaker. She hosts the *Suze Orman Show*, which airs on CNBC. Communications coach and business writer Carmine Gallo profiled Suze Orman in a March 2013 article for *Forbes*. He wrote that one of the keys to Orman's success is simplicity:

> Orman doesn't speak in the jargon so common in the financial industry. She speaks simply. More important, she has the courage to speak simply and that makes all the difference. "Too many people want to impress others with information so others think the speaker is intelligent. All I care about is that the information empowers the viewer or the reader," Orman said.
>
> "But Suze, if your message is too simple, don't you risk not being taken seriously?" I asked.

"Here's the key. You must not be afraid of criticism," Orman said. "If your intention is to impart a message that will create change for the person listening, then if you ask me it's respectful to that person to make the message as simple as possible. Some people criticize simplicity because they think their jobs could be eliminated. It's our fear of extinction, our fear of elimination, our fear of not being important that leads us to communicate things in a more complex way than we need to."[20]

The most successful people in business will tell you that simplicity is a powerful success principle. One of the leading proponents of simplicity in the business world is Jack Welch. During his tenure as chairman and CEO of General Electric (from 1981 to 2001), the value of GE soared 4,000 percent. He once observed, "People always overestimate how complex business is. This isn't rocket science. We've chosen one of the world's simplest professions."[21] In his 1995 "Letter to Share Owners" in the *General Electric Annual Report*, Welch explained why simplicity is the best business policy: "Simple messages travel faster, simpler designs reach the market faster, and the elimination of clutter allows faster decision making."[22]

A prime illustration of the power of simplicity in business is Henry Ford's Model T car. The Ford Motor Company produced more than fifteen million Model Ts from September 1908 to October 1927. It was the first car that was designed to be affordable by middle-class Americans. Because of its success, Henry Ford's Model T was named the "car of the century" by the Global Automotive Elections Foundation in 1999.[23]

Why was the Model T so successful? Simplicity. In *America, 1908*, journalist-historian Jim Rasenberger explains:

> Every aspect of the car was considered with an eye to simplicity, inside and out. The simpler a piece of machinery, Ford understood, the lower the cost of manufacturing it, and the easier and cheaper the task of maintaining it. Equipped with a manual

and a few basic tools, a Model T owner would be able to carry out most repairs himself. The new car's planetary transmission would be smoother and longer lasting than any that had ever been designed. The magneto, a small magnetized generator that provided a steady flash of voltage to ignite the automobile's fuel, would be more dependable.

More obvious were the bodily changes on the exterior, those characteristics that made it appear so ungainly at first sight. The Model T was designed to ride high off the ground to give it plenty of clearance over America's infamously bumpy roadways, while the car's three-point suspension system allowed it to handle the roads without tossing its occupants into a roadside ditch.[24]

So if you want to be successful, effective, and influential, if you want to impact the marketplace or impact your world, keep it simple. Resist the temptation to dazzle people with your complex words and ideas. Show how brilliant you *really* are through your mastery of simplicity.

"Just a Simple Farm Boy"

In August 1993, John MacArthur, noted pastor and president of Master's College in Southern California, received a phone call. The soft-spoken, humble-sounding voice on the line said, "Hello, I'm John Wooden, and I used to be a basketball coach at UCLA. I understand Bill Oates is under consideration for the head coaching job at your school, and I think he'd be perfect for that position. From the standpoint of his preparation as a coach, and from the standpoint of his being a strong Christian, I highly recommend Bill." Bill Oates got the job.

Bill once told me that much of Coach Wooden's greatness was attributable to his simplicity, which was rooted in his humility. "Success never changed Coach Wooden," Bill said. "In 2003, he went to the White House to receive the Presidential Medal of Freedom from President Bush. Afterward, Coach Wooden told me, 'I couldn't believe I was there. I am just a simple farm boy.' He has remained untouched by all his success."

It's true. That "simple farm boy" just happened to be the greatest coach who ever lived and didn't even seem to be aware of it. He thought of himself in simple terms, he taught the game of basketball and the game of life through simple principles and maxims, he lived simply, he communicated simply, and he was simply a great human being.

In 1962, two years before Coach Wooden's UCLA Bruins won their first NCAA title, they came up short, losing to Cincinnati in the first round of the Final Four—a heartbreaking two-point loss. Afterward, Coach Wooden spent a lot of time analyzing the loss. After a time of reflection, he concluded that there was no one to blame but himself.

He later explained:

> When UCLA qualified for the NCAA postseason tournament, I intensified our already grueling practices, working players even harder—so hard, in fact, that by tournament time they were physically and mentally spent. . . . I added new plays and piled on more information. Instead of staying with what had worked during the regular season—a clear and uncomplicated strategy— I intentionally made things complicated. I resolved that in the future I would keep it simple going into postseason play just as I did during the regular season.[25]

That loss in 1962 taught Coach Wooden the importance of maintaining an uncomplicated approach to teaching and coaching his players. It was simplicity that got them to the Final Four, and in the years that followed, it was simplicity that got them to a string of NCAA championships. Coach Wooden learned the lesson of defeat: in the game of basketball, as in every other field of endeavor, simplicity is a virtue.

Len Elmore played for eight years in the NBA before going on to a career in broadcasting and law. Though he never played for Coach Wooden (he graduated from Maryland), Len was a big fan and avid student of Coach Wooden and his coaching philosophy. Len told me, "John Wooden is the most remarkable, uncomplicated genius ever. Everything he teaches and does is so basic. It just comes down to using common sense. His phrase, 'Be quick but don't hurry'—I refer to that all the time. Coach Wooden teaches us that there's no substitute for paying attention to the smallest detail. Then, when you stack one detail on top of the other, you build a strong foundation for getting the maximum from your abilities."

Here, then, are a few lessons on how to achieve greater success through simplification:

- *Simplicity is the key to effective teaching.* Great teachers, like Coach Wooden, are great simplifiers. They take complex ideas or skills, break them down into their component parts, then teach them one simple piece at a time. Then they gradually add new ideas or new skills, one at a time, drill them repeatedly, and enable students to gradually achieve mastery without being overwhelmed by complexity.

- *Become immune to criticism.* If you take a simplified approach, people may criticize you for not being "sophisticated," for not having any "trick plays," for not having any "complex strategies." Don't let the critics tempt you to stray from your wise strategy of keeping it simple. The best answer to any critic is success. And simplicity is the key to success.

- *Simple sayings are simply powerful.* Coach Wooden used his maxims (or "Woodenisms") to make his lessons memorable. Decades later, his former students still draw from the wisdom of those sayings. Use Coach Wooden's concise expressions of wisdom to motivate yourself and others.

Devise simple maxims of your own. Become a source of simple but powerful wisdom for the people around you.

- *Simplicity is the key to victory in any competitive endeavor.* The bitter experience of General Eisenhower and Operation Market Garden demonstrates that we should always listen to our instincts for simplicity. Complexity produces confusion. Simplicity produces clarity and confidence. When you compete against an opponent, you want your opponent to be confused, and you want all your own people to be on the same page. Eliminate as many complex variables as you can. Leave complexity to your opponent. To be victorious, keep it simple.

- *Set goals that are so clear and simple that everyone can be inspired and motivated by them.* Successful organizations set goals that can be translated into slogans. IBM founder Thomas Watson had a goal of utilizing the collective *brainpower* of his workforce, so he posted a simple slogan all around the company: "Think." Apple founder Steve Jobs had a different goal; he wanted to utilize the collective *creativity* of his workforce, so he posted the slogan "Think Different." Successful leaders keep their goals simple—and make sure everyone in the organization knows the goals. In your leadership role, make sure your message is simple, memorable, and draws your organization closer to your goals.

- *When planning, keep your plans simple and flexible.* Coach Vince Lombardi believed that when a plan failed, it was usually because the plan was too complicated to learn in a limited amount of time. The best plan is a simple plan that you and your people can practice and rehearse until it becomes automatic and instinctive.

- *Communicate simply.* Remove jargon and multisyllabic obfuscation from your speech and writing. Say everything simply so that everyone can understand. Say it passionately so that everyone will feel your energy. Resist the temptation to impress others with big words and flowery speech. Communicate to influence and inspire, not to impress.

- *Never confuse "simple" with "easy."* The simplest solutions are seldom easy but are usually the most effective solutions. In fact, those times when problems seem the most difficult to solve are the times when you need to communicate solutions in the simplest way possible. Simply state the problem, then simply state the options, with their respective advantages and drawbacks. By reducing the problem to its simple essence, the solution often becomes abundantly clear. As Jack Welch observed, "The elimination of clutter allows faster decision making."

As Coach Wooden himself put it so well, "Keep things as simple as you can and you have a chance to do them better. I'd always rather do a few things well."[26]

3

Little Things Prepare You for Great Things

Never try to be better than someone else. Learn from others, and try to be the best you can be. Success is the by-product of that preparation.

Coach John Wooden

Ralph Drollinger played for UCLA from 1972 to 1976, but a promising NBA career was cut short after only six games with the Dallas Mavericks because of a severe knee injury. Drollinger went on to help found Sports Outreach America and *Sports Spectrum* magazine. He also produced *Julius Erving's Sports Focus*, a weekly half-hour show on ESPN. Ralph once told me a story that speaks volumes about the importance of paying attention to the little things as a part of preparing for future success.

"In my first year at UCLA in 1972," he said, "freshmen were deemed eligible to play on the varsity team. So I found myself practicing with Bill Walton and the other great players of that era. Being on the right team at the right time with the right coach, I had the privilege of becoming the first player to go to the NCAA Final Four Tournament four years in a row. During one of those practices, I learned a lesson I will never forget.

"In the practice, I grabbed a defensive rebound, then turned to make my outlet pass to the guard waiting near the sideline, just this side of half court. But I was careless and threw the outlet pass away—it was intercepted. So Coach Wooden blew his whistle, stopped the practice, and very kindly instructed me in front of my teammates, 'Ralph, you must not throw away the outlet pass.'

"'Yes, sir,' I replied.

"Half an hour later, I did it again—threw another outlet pass away. Coach stopped the practice again. This time, his tone was noticeably more stern as he said, 'Ralph, do you know *why* you are not to throw away the outlet pass?'

"I recited the philosophy of a fast-break offense and the numerical advantage that a team either gains or loses, depending on the successful completion of the outlet pass. Coach seemed satisfied that I at least understood what I needed to do and why I needed to do it. So the practice continued.

"In the final minutes of the practice, the unthinkable happened. For the third time, I threw away the outlet pass. Coach blasted his whistle three times, like a train pulling out of the station. Everything stopped. Coach sat me down on the half-court paint. With my teammates surrounding me, Coach delivered a strict admonition: 'Ralph, if you ever throw away another outlet pass, you will be denied the privilege of practicing with your teammates.'

"I was beginning to get the message. Coach Wooden wanted me to be thoroughly prepared when I got out on the court in a real game. He didn't want to see me throw away an outlet pass in a pressure situation. He didn't want these mistakes to turn into habits that would cost our team a game. I learned then and there a lesson I've carried throughout my career and my Christian life: When preparing for success, focus on the little things, focus on the fundamentals. Be faithful in doing the little things well so that you can one day hear the Master say, 'Well done, good and faithful servant.'"

George Morgan was a student manager for the Bruins during Coach Wooden's tenure. He recalls that Coach Wooden "had his teams as well prepared as anybody. His teams were so well prepared that it was hard for them to lose. It was the emphasis on fundamentals and doing simple things right all the time."

Coach Wooden believed that a coach should prepare his players before the game, then, on game night, the coach should step back and let the players play their game. As Coach Wooden himself observed:

> We coaches try to get involved too much during a game. It seems that players spend too much of their time watching the bench for hand, towel, or card signals that call for a change in offense or defense.
>
> I think the coach's job is to prepare players to play and then let them do it. Failure to prepare is preparing to fail. And the preparation process has to take place before the game, with any needed adjustments made during time-outs and at half time.[1]

One of the ways Coach Wooden prepared his players was by making sure they were in top physical condition and were capable of delivering a peak performance for a full forty-minute game. He wrote:

> I remember so well a comment made during our NCAA Final in 1975 against Kentucky by Billy Packer, the television analyst. He said that Kentucky would "wear UCLA down" because I was not substituting and resting my players. But I knew they were in top condition, and at the end of the game I believe most

observers would have said that my players were running faster, jumping higher, and executing better than our opposition. . . .

If my players were physically and emotionally fit and were prepared for the game, they could play good basketball for the entire game. So I never went in for the razzle-dazzle of running players on and off the court during the game.[2]

Writing in *Investor's Business Daily*, business writer Michael Mink observes that, for Coach Wooden, the process of preparation was far more important than a focus on winning. "My thoughts were directed toward preparation, our journey," Coach Wooden said, "not the results of the effort." And John Wooden's biographer, Steve Jamison, told Mink, "Winning is a by-product. . . . That concept is absolutely key, and it is a key distinction between John Wooden's philosophy and [the vast majority] of other coaches."

Mink concluded, "Preparation, strict adherence to details and a work ethic, with which Wooden led by example, were the tools of his title trade. Details, the coach wrote, 'are fundamental to your progress in basketball, business and life. They are the difference between champions and near champions.'"[3]

"No Such Thing as a Small Error"

Whether you are an athlete or an artist, a CEO, or a college grad looking for a job, you must prepare yourself for success. And preparation is a matter of focusing on the little things.

Og Mandino was the author of the bestselling book *The Greatest Salesman in the World* and president of *Success Unlimited* magazine. He once wrote about the importance of the little things when preparing for success:

There are hundreds of stories stressing the importance of little things. A door left unopened, a document unsigned, a few live coals left upon a hearth; Edison losing a patent because of a misplaced decimal point. Vital battles have been lost for the "want of a nail." We grow sentimental over songs that tell us "It's the little things that count," but we go right on disregarding the little things.

At a prayer meeting in an old country church, a pious member was overheard imploring fervently, "Use me, O Lord, use me—but in an executive capacity." . . . The truth is that no man, no job, is little. Men and jobs are different: easier to handle, or easier to approach, or with a less significant result. But everything that requires noticing or doing is big. . . .

The good executive keeps his finger on the little things: he knows that they may, if mishandled, become big problems. To an operating surgeon there are no little things: every slightest detail is a matter of life and death. To a lawyer, an obscure and minute legal confusion may cost a client liberty, even life. . . . We must appreciate the details; we must *care* for them.[4]

Kareem Abdul-Jabbar is the NBA's all-time leading scorer with 38,387 points. Prior to his NBA career with the Milwaukee Bucks and Los Angeles Lakers, Kareem played for Coach Wooden and the Bruins. He helped lift his teams to three consecutive NCAA championships and six NBA championships. Recalling the lessons he learned from Coach Wooden, Kareem once said, "I try to do the right thing at the right time. They may just be little things, but usually they make the difference between winning and losing."[5]

Paul "Bear" Bryant, longtime head football coach of the University of Alabama Crimson Tide, once said that the preparation for success requires an intense focus on the details and the fundamentals. "Little things make the difference," he said. "Everyone is well-prepared in the big things, but only the winners perfect the little things."[6]

Don Shula coached the Miami Dolphins to two Super Bowl victories and the NFL's only perfect season. He holds the NFL record for most career wins (347) and the most Super Bowl appearances as head coach (6). Bob Griese, who quarterbacked the Dolphins during the undefeated season, told Curt Schleier of *Investor's Business Daily* that when Don Shula took over as head coach of the Dolphins in 1970, he focused on preparation. "You've heard of two-a-days," Griese said. "We did four-a-days."[7]

My writing partner, Jim Denney, who worked with Bob Griese on his book *Undefeated*, tells me that Griese described Shula's workouts as "football boot camp," adding that he had never worked harder in his life. "Shula had the Dolphins do scrimmages, seven-on-sevens, Oklahoma drills, and 'gassers.' They'd run gassers at the end of every practice. Shula broke the team into squads, and each squad would sprint from sideline to sideline and back again, rest thirty seconds, run it again, rest thirty seconds, and run it a third time. They had to sprint flat out every time. Shula ran the gassers with them."

Griese recalled that his teammates complained about the intensity of the workouts, "but when we were tested and did well, they started to give credit to the hard work and preparation."[8] One of the biggest tests came on Christmas Day 1971, a divisional play-off game against the Kansas City Chiefs. The Dolphins battled the Chiefs to a 24–24 tie at the end of regulation play. When the first overtime period failed to decide the game, they went into a second overtime. At that point, the Dolphins realized they still had plenty of stamina, while Kansas City was tiring. Shula's Dolphins were the better-conditioned team, thanks to the intense preparation Coach Shula had put them through. The Dolphins won the game in the second overtime with a field goal from the thirty-yard line. Shula and the Dolphins went on to Super Bowl VI, and though they lost to Dallas, it was the first of three consecutive Super Bowl appearances—and the Dolphins won Super Bowls VII and VIII.

Bob Griese told Curt Schleier that he and his teammates at-tributed much of their success to Shula's attention to detail, his focus on the little things while preparing his team for victory. Schleier writes that Shula "would stop workouts for what oth-ers might perceive as minor errors. 'If a guy jumped off sides in practice, I'd use that as an example,' Shula said. 'I'd stop the practice and say if this happened in a critical part of the game and we got penalized because you didn't know the snap count, it could affect the play. It could affect the game. I always made them understand that there was no such thing as a small error or small mistake. . . . I always tried to have my practices fast-paced and everything done at full speed and as close to game condi-tions as I could possibly make them. . . . That better prepared the players for the game.'"[9]

Preparation, Shula recalled, was the result of a lot of little things done well. "I think every coach walks into a room," Shula told Curt Schleier, "and the first thing he says is that our goal this year is to win the Super Bowl. But you have to be sure you're willing to do the little things to help put you in a position to reach your goal."[10]

That Little Extra Edge

One of my greatest heroes when I was growing up was Ted Williams. During his nineteen seasons with the Boston Red Sox (interrupted by service in World War II), he led the league in batting for six seasons and retired with 521 career home runs. When he batted .406 in 1941, Williams became the last major league player to bat over .400 in a season.

I became acquainted with Ted Williams after I moved to Or-lando. Williams had founded the Hitters Hall of Fame at the Ted Williams Museum, now located at Tropicana Field in St. Peters-burg, Florida, home of the Tampa Bay Rays. Many years ago, I began attending the induction ceremonies held every February. There would be a dinner and a presentation, and many of my boyhood heroes would be there. It was like visiting a baseball Valhalla, and Williams himself was always the main attraction.

At one of these dinners, a fan brought with him a well-worn baseball bat. He showed it to Williams and said, "I've had this bat for a long time. I'm told that you used it in 1941, the season you hit .406."

Williams held the bat in his hands, closed his eyes, and tightened his hands around the grip. Then he smiled. "Yep," he said, "this is one of my bats. In 1940 and '41, I'd make a groove in the handle for my right index finger to nestle in. I feel that groove. Yep, this is definitely one of my bats."

That little groove speaks volumes about Williams's commitment to preparation—and to the fact that, even after sixty years, it was still the little things that mattered. Those who knew Williams well in his playing days remember his intense preparation and his attention to the little things. Writer Ally Rogers adds these insights into Williams's extreme focus on the little things—including the tiniest aspects of his special-order, hand-crafted bats:

> Most MLB [Major League Baseball] players prefer hand-crafted bats. Ted Williams regularly tipped Fitz Bickle $10, a chunk of money in the 1930s, to be his personal hand-turner [bat maker] after several mistakes were made by other turners.
>
> Aaron Gaddie, a tour guide at the Slugger Museum and Factory, explained that Williams came to the factory when it was located off East Broadway. He was given three bats—one was half-an-ounce heavier than the others. Williams immediately picked it out and gave it back. Later, Williams was sent a set of bats, which ended up being 5/1000th of an inch bigger in diameter than his others. He sent them back. Each Williams bat had to have eight to ten grain lines per inch, or it was sent back.[11]

Like Williams, second baseman Bobby Doerr played his entire career for the Red Sox. He recalls being impressed with Williams's intense focus on the little things when it came to his bats. On one occasion during spring training, the Red Sox were in Kentucky to play an exhibition game against their Louisville farm club. Doerr remembers that the night before the game, Williams suggested that he and his teammates go to the Louisville factory where the bats were made.

So early the next morning, the Red Sox went to the factory and got a tour. Williams paused to talk to an older gentleman who was turning bats at the lathe. "Anytime you find any little pin knots in wood," Williams told him, handing him a twenty-dollar bill, "put 'em in my bat."[12] Those little pin knots formed hard spots in the wood, giving the bat just a little extra kick, a tiny percentage of added power. Yet all those little things that Williams focused on added up to a big difference in his batting average.

Jack Fadden, a trainer for both Harvard University and the Red Sox in the 1950s, offered these insights about Williams's attention to detail:

> He studies every player, every park. He knows the slant of the batter's box. . . . He knows the height of every pitcher's mound. He knows the throwing power of every outfielder. I found that out one day when he made a hit to right-center.
>
> He ambled down to first, almost to the point of seeming lazy. The next day, with a new club in town, he hit, ran to first, and made the turn at first. It was almost the exact same hit on the very same spot. Why the difference? Ted explained to me about the two outfielders who handled the ball. One was a rockhead; the other was ready and able to throw him out if he didn't hustle. He knows when to conserve energy. . . .
>
> Williams doesn't hit just because of what he does that day. It's his advance preparation. . . . His sweatshirts have to fit just right. He breaks in shoes a year in advance. You've seen him tug

and twist a cap. That's to make it fit just so. A poor fit might distract him. He'll rip out a worn shoe lacing. Right down to the smallest detail, everything has to be just right. Nothing must interfere. He makes sure of that.[13]

Mediocre achievers are content with mediocre preparation. They dismiss the little things as unimportant details. But great achievers such as Williams understand that all those little things add up. Cumulatively, they become that little extra edge that spells the difference between good and great.

The Rewards Go to the Best Prepared

What's true of success in basketball, football, and baseball is true in every field of endeavor. In order to succeed, you must prepare for success. And the key to preparation is paying careful attention to the little things.

Are you in the job market, competing against other candidates for that dream job? Then you'd better be thoroughly prepared, and you'd better make sure you have mastered all the little things that will give you an edge over your competitors. Remember, the job doesn't always go to the person most qualified. It generally goes to the one who is best prepared.

As you conduct your job search, pay attention to all the little things that will give you an edge. Take time to research prospective employers so that you can talk intelligently about their company and their marketplace during the interview. Don't try too hard to impress with your knowledge; just be prepared to interact in a competent and well-informed way.

Make sure that your email, voice mail, website, and social network postings project professionalism and competence. Prospective employers will often look at your internet and social network activities, so make sure there is nothing online that can embarrass you or hurt your chances to get that job.

When you go into a job interview, be aware that employers see many candidates with similar levels of education, experience, and other qualifications on their résumé. There will probably not be one big thing in your interview that will set you apart from the other candidates. The employer will probably make a decision based on a lot of little things that take place during the interview.

One of the best ways to give yourself an edge in an interview is to arrive early. An early arrival for your interview signals that you are trustworthy, diligent, and considerate of the employer's time. Successful people value their time, and they appreciate it when you value their time as well. Arriving late will brand you as someone who is undisciplined and irresponsible.

Plan to arrive early so that you have some leeway in case of an unforeseen delay. If you give yourself only enough time to arrive for your appointment right on the dot, you are setting yourself up to be late. Even if you arrive on time, you'll probably be stressed and hurried. Instead of focusing on what you need to do and say in the interview, you'll be mentally rehearsing excuses for your tardiness. You never have to make an excuse for being early.

Once you arrive, continually ask yourself, Am I making a good first impression? Am I smiling? Does my voice sound strong and confident? Do I make eye contact? Do I call my prospective employer by name (for example, Mr. Johnson or Ms. Jones)? Do I seem relaxed and at ease? Do I answer questions thoroughly yet concisely and with a clear grasp of what I'm being asked? Or do I seem nervous, evasive, or guarded, as if I'm hiding something?

These are a few of the many little things that can make a big difference in your chances of getting a job. Make sure you have prepared yourself well by paying close attention to the little things.

A number of years ago, a business magazine suggested that there is a marked difference between the business culture on the East Coast of America and the culture on the West Coast. The East Coast is more buttoned-down and formal, while the West Coast business culture is more loose and laid-back. The reason for the difference, this magazine claimed, is a difference in preparation for disasters.

On the East Coast, disasters have seasons. Hurricanes and blizzards are seasonal events. People on the East Coast expect hurricanes during hurricane season and blizzards during blizzard season, and they prepare accordingly. They know how to protect themselves and their property, and they are always prepared for the annual onslaught.

But on the West Coast, the most common disaster is an earthquake, and there is no such thing as earthquake season. You can plan for earthquakes to a certain extent, but you never know when one is coming, how strong it will be, or how much damage it will do. Earthquakes strike without warning, so you have to be flexible, adaptable, and ready to deal with the unexpected at any moment. As a result, the culture on the West Coast has a higher tolerance for uncertainty, informality, chaos, and change.

There is nothing wrong with either the East Coast or the West Coast approach. In fact, the wisest businesspeople are those who adopt the attitudes of *both* coasts. Whatever business you're in, no matter what endeavors you engage in, make plans for the predictable, recurring problems. Be prepared to protect yourself and your business against seasonal crises. But also be flexible and adaptable enough to handle the occasional unscheduled earthquake-type disasters. Expect the unexpected. Don't let chaos and change throw you.

Prepare well for the disasters you expect. Prepare even more thoroughly for the disasters you don't expect. And you prepare by mastering the little things.

Good News for Lug Nuts

If you want to succeed in life, you need to be prepared for success. Here are some principles to master as you prepare yourself and your organization:

- *Prepare your people for success, then let them do their jobs.* Preparation, Coach Wooden said, should take place before the game. Any adjustments that need to be made should take place during time-outs and halftime. If you are in a leadership role, make sure you prepare your people well—then step back and watch them succeed!

- *Winning is not the objective; winning is a by-product.* Winning is the result of preparation, a strong work ethic, and careful attention to the little things.

- *Winners understand that there is no such thing as a small mistake.* The tiniest error can lead to a major setback. Anyone can say, "Our goal is to win the championship." But true champions say, "We are going to eliminate all the little mistakes that could cost us the championship."

- *There is no one big secret to success.* There are only a lot of little things that add up to a slight edge. Ted Williams was concerned about the precise weight and thickness of his bats, the number of grain lines per inch, the number of little pin knots in the wood, the slant of the batter's box, the height of the pitcher's mound, the throwing power of the outfielders, the fit of his shoes and shirts and cap, and on and on. They were all little things, and no single detail could give him the winning edge—but all of them together added up to the difference between good and great.

- *The rewards go to the best prepared.* Whether you are a CEO, an employee, or a job seeker, there are hundreds of little things you can do to prepare yourself for success. "Good enough" is never good enough. Identify all the little things you can do to give yourself and your company a little edge over the competition. Do them conscientiously and consistently, and no matter what business you're in, you will become the Ted Williams or Coach Wooden of that endeavor.

- *Be prepared for anything.* Prepare yourself for the problems, crises, and disasters you expect, the problems that occur on a regular basis. And prepare yourself for the unexpected catastrophe. Have contingency plans ready and try to foresee the unforeseeable.

- *Remember, there are no unimportant people, no little roles.* If you are a leader, make sure everyone in your organization is prepared to step in, work hard, and achieve great results. Prepare your subs as well as your starters. And if you are a player, do everything you can to prepare for the day your coach or your leader calls your number and sends you into the game. Someday your chance will come to prove yourself. Make sure you are well prepared for that opportunity.

Coach Wooden often shared an analogy with his players. It's an analogy about the importance of the total team effort. Coach wanted his players to know that the subs were just as important as the starters, the role players were just as important as the stars. He recalled:

> I told players at UCLA that we, as a team, are like a powerful car. Maybe a Bill Walton or Kareem Abdul-Jabbar . . . is the big engine, but if one wheel is flat, we're going no place. And if we have brand-new tires but the lug nuts are missing, the wheels come off. What good is a powerful engine now? It's no good at all.
>
> A lug nut may seem like a little thing, but it's not. There's a role that each and every one of us must play. We may aspire to what we consider to be a larger role, or a more important role, but we cannot achieve that until we show that we are able to fulfill the role we are assigned. It's these little things that make the big things happen. . . .

Of course, when I told the players about their roles and the car with the powerful engine, new tires, and tight lug nuts, I also reminded them the car needed a driver behind the wheel or it would just go around in circles or smash into a tree.

I told them the driver was me.[14]

If you are in a leadership role—whether in a company, a church, a team, or a family—part of your job is to prepare your people for success. Help them see that there are no small roles. A lug nut may seem like a little thing compared to a roaring engine, but little things like lug nuts are crucial to excellent performance. Prepare yourself and your people for victory, then step confidently onto the field of competition and achieve your dreams.

4

Little Things Are the Key to Achieving Your Goals

Success is peace of mind which is a direct result of self-satisfaction in knowing you did your best to become the best you are capable of becoming.

Coach John Wooden

LYNN SHACKELFORD PLAYED BASKETBALL AT UCLA for Coach John Wooden, had a brief pro basketball career, then went into sports broadcasting. He tells a story that illustrates Coach Wooden's genius for identifying the little things a player can do to better reach his personal and team goals.

Shackelford recalls that Coach Wooden "had a Master's degree in English and can say in one or two sentences what it takes most coaches five minutes to say. A great example is when I was a 75 percent free throw shooter in high school. One day after my freshman year [at UCLA], he comes up and says I should be a much better free throw shooter because I could make every jump shot from the same spot. He told me not to take too much time bouncing and dribbling. Just do it."

So Shackelford took Coach Wooden's advice. Instead of bouncing the ball and trying to psych himself up to shoot the free throw, he would simply step up to the line and shoot. The result? "I was over 80 percent for most of the next year."[1]

Coach Wooden understood that it's important to set big goals, but he also knew that the key to reaching those big goals lies in caring about the little things.

Born on his parents' farm near Centerville, Indiana, "Johnny" Wooden learned to play basketball in his little rural elementary school. After his parents lost the farm and moved into the town of Martinsville, Johnny became a star player on his high school team, leading the team to the state championship game in all three of his years there.

The game of basketball has a near-religious grip on the people of Indiana. "Everybody there is crazy over basketball," Coach Wooden once told an interviewer, adding that in those days the little town of Martinsville "had 4,800 people, and yet they had built a gymnasium the year before I entered high school that seated 5,200 and it was always full."[2]

Wooden entered Purdue University to study engineering but soon switched his major to English. Playing basketball for the Purdue Boilermakers, Wooden quickly became known as a fearless guard whose suicide dives after loose balls earned him the nickname "Indiana Rubber Man." He made all-American three years in a row.

After graduation in 1932, John Wooden turned down a chance to play professional basketball for the Boston Celtics, preferring a teaching career instead. He spent eleven years teaching English and coaching basketball at South Bend Central High School in

Indiana, winning 218 games while losing only 42. After a stint in the navy during World War II, he taught and coached at Indiana State Teachers' College (now Indiana State University), where he racked up more winning seasons.

After accepting the head coaching job at UCLA in 1948, he turned one of the worst teams in the NCAA into a powerhouse, winning 22 of 29 games in his first season. Over a forty-year coaching career, Coach Wooden compiled a record of 885 wins, 203 losses, ten national championships, and a winning percentage of .813. Coach Wooden attributed the achievement of these lofty goals not to any single big thing he did but to a lot of little things done well. He observed:

> High performance and production are achieved only through the identification and perfection of small but relevant details—little things done well. Sloppiness in tending to details is common in sports as well as other types of organizations. When it occurs, blame rests with you, the leader, not with your team. Those under your leadership must be taught that little things make the big things happen. In fact, they must first learn there are no big things, only a logical accumulation of little things done at a very high standard of performance.
>
> I derived great satisfaction from identifying and perfecting those "trivial" and often troublesome details, because I knew, without doubt, that each one brought UCLA a bit closer to our goal: competitive greatness. If you collect enough pennies you'll eventually be rich. Each relevant and perfect detail was another penny in our bank.[3]

Through his extraordinary record of achievement, Coach John Wooden proved that the way to achieve dauntingly high goals is through a relentless focus on achieving optimal performance in a lot of seemingly little things. Those little things accumulate over time and make a big difference.

Do Little Things Every Day

What is the goal you dream of accomplishing? Do you picture yourself writing the great American novel? That's a worthwhile goal. What steps have you taken, what little things have you done, to start moving toward the achievement of that goal? Writing a novel is not something you sit down and do one Sunday afternoon when you have some free time. A novel is a result of many individual steps, many little things done well. You have to come up with a plot, imagine a cast of characters, figure out how to get those characters into conflict with one another, and build a habit of writing a few pages every day. After you've written your first draft, you have to refine it through additional drafts, then find an agent and a publisher. Once it's published, there are still many little things you must continue to do well in order to promote your great American novel to the public.

If you don't believe me, ask novelist Brandi Bates, author of *Remains to Be Seen*. As she once said, "Do little things every day that no one else seems to want to do, be patient, and success will find you."[4] Or as James Jones, author of *From Here to Eternity*, once put it, writing a novel is simple: "Just write one page every day and at the end of the year you've got a 365-page book."[5] Do little things well every day—that's good advice for achieving any lofty goal in life.

David Schwartz was a university professor and motivational writer, best known for his book *The Magic of Thinking Big* (1959). Schwartz also founded a leadership consultancy firm called Creative Educational Services, Inc. In his book, Schwartz wrote, "The person determined to achieve maximum success learns the principle that progress is made one step at a time. A house is built one brick at a time. Football games are won a play at a time. A department store grows bigger one customer at a time. Every big accomplishment is a series of little accomplishments."[6]

Schwartz goes on to tell the story of newsman Eric Sevareid. As a war correspondent during World War II, Sevareid was forced to parachute, along with several airmen, from a crippled transport plane over Burma. Sevareid and his companions landed in mountainous territory amid steamy August monsoon rains. Civilization lay at the end of a 140-mile march to neighboring India. In the first hour of his trek, Sevareid suffered a puncture wound from a boot nail; within hours, he had huge blisters on both feet.

Sevareid recalled the thought process that got him and his companions through that seemingly impossible journey: "Could I hobble 140 miles? Could the others, some in worse shape than I, complete such a distance? We were convinced we could not. But we *could* hobble to that ridge, we *could* make the next friendly village for the night. And that, of course, was all we had to do."[7]

Every journey to a goal is the result of a lot of incremental steps, a lot of small objectives met, a lot of little things done well. Whatever your trek to success may be, you probably can't reach it in a single leap. But you can hobble to the next ridge. You can make it to the next friendly village. And step-by-step, you can reach your "impossible" goal.

Nido Qubein came to America from Lebanon in 1966, arriving with only fifty dollars in his pocket. He taught himself English and eventually became a successful entrepreneur, author, and speaker. Today, he is the president of High Point University in North Carolina and the author of eleven books. Qubein is also a founder of the National Speakers Association Foundation, and he sits on the boards of several major companies. He observed, "One of the greatest reasons people cannot mobilize themselves is that they try to accomplish great things. Most worthwhile achievements are the result of many little things done in a single direction."[8]

Wangari Muta Maathai was a Kenyan environmentalist and founder of the Green Belt Movement, an environmental nongovernmental organization focused on global conservation. Beginning in the 1970s, she worked tirelessly to combat deforestation, desertification, water shortages, and hunger throughout Africa and the Third World. She also fought for women's rights and democracy in nations ruled by oppressive dictatorships.

In 1992, Maathai learned that she and fellow activists had been targeted for assassination by a cabal within the government. She barricaded herself inside her home behind iron bars. Outside, the police laid siege to her house. After three days, the police finally cut through the bars, entered her home, and arrested her. Maathai and other activists were charged with treason. When American lawmakers and a variety of international organizations demanded that the Kenyan government prove the charges against Maathai, the government backed down and dropped the charges. In 2004, she was awarded the Nobel Peace Prize for her "contribution to sustainable development, democracy and peace"—the first African woman to be so honored. She died in 2011.

Maathai once said, "It's the little things citizens do. That's what will make the difference. My little thing is planting trees." The "little things" she did made a big difference in the world.[9]

Madan Birla is president of Innovation Culture Group and author of *FedEx Delivers*. He spent twenty-two years at Federal Express, working closely with company founder Fred Smith. In his book, he explains why Federal Express pursued a goal of 100 percent customer satisfaction:

> "A Satisfied Customer Made This Possible." That phrase is printed at the front of FedEx paycheck envelopes to remind all employees that satisfying the customer is everyone's responsibility. The phrase makes the goal clear: 100 percent customer satisfaction after every interaction and transaction, and 100 percent service performance, ensuring that all deliveries are

made within the time commitment for the service selected by the customer. . . .

Employees from at least five departments physically handle a domestic package between pickup and delivery. Even a 99 percent service level for each would result in only 95 percent of the customers receiving the package on time. With 3 million packages flowing through the system every night, 99 percent translates to 30,000 unhappy customers per day.[10]

Most people would consider a 99 percent success rate to be absolutely phenomenal. FedEx considers a 99 percent success rate to be nothing short of dismal. The company expects all its people to deliver that last 1 percent of accuracy, efficiency, and customer satisfaction. How about you? Do you expect a 100 percent performance from yourself 100 percent of the time? If not, why not?

Coach Wooden's focus on the little things, from correctly putting on socks to the best form for shooting free throws, was devoted to getting that 1 percent of effectiveness from his teams. That last 1 percent of performance usually gave his teams the winning edge. As legendary NFL coach Vince Lombardi put it, "Inches make a champion."[11]

Lose the Detail, Lose It All

Jim Calhoun coached the University of Connecticut men's basketball team to three national championships—1999, 2004, and 2011. He retired in 2012 with a career record of 866 wins, 369 losses, and a .701 winning percentage. Jim is the author of *A Passion to Lead*. In that book, he wrote:

What is a basketball game? It's really a long series of little battles played out over forty minutes, hundreds of momentary skirmishes—battles for loose balls and rebounds, one-on-one matchups between a guy who, with the shot clock running down, is going to shoot the ball and a defender who must keep him from putting it in the basket. Win enough of those little fights and you win the game. You've got a few more points on the scoreboard than your opponent when the final horn sounds. By doing lots of little things well, you've accomplished a very big goal.[12]

I'm a great admirer of Walt Disney, and I have written two books on his life and his philosophy. Walt was fascinated with the little things that make big things happen. Though he dreamed on the grandest scale imaginable, he always paid careful attention to the tiniest details. When he was building the world's first theme park in 1955, Walt said, "The thing that's going to make Disneyland unique and different is the detail. If we lose the detail, we lose it all."[13]

And in the 1960s, as he was planning his second theme park in central Florida, there was one little spot at the center of his grand architectural plan, and he would point to that spot and say, "There's going to be a spot right here with a little bench. That's where Lilly and I are going to sit and watch it being built."[14] Even though Walt Disney had a vast goal in mind, he had that little detail, that little bench in the center of it all that was going to be his vantage point.

When I interviewed Walt's grandson Walter Disney Miller, he told me, "People who worked with my grandpa say that he seemed to be everywhere at once and he never forgot anything. He could remember things people did or said a decade or two earlier—and he would remember it in exact detail."

Disney historian Michael Broggie, the son of Walt's first imagineer, Roger Broggie, told me, "When I was a kid of eight or nine, I loved to visit Walt's office. I'd go to his office door, and if he wasn't too busy, he'd say, 'Michael, come in, let's talk!' I'd sit in a chair, and he'd start grilling me. 'What are you watching on TV? What are you reading?' He was probing for detailed information on what my generation liked and enjoyed. He was doing market research."

Walt Disney's practiced eye never missed a detail. One time, his animation staff produced some footage of a Mickey Mouse cartoon for Walt's approval. Just to test Walt, they cut the tail off Mickey in a single frame of the cartoon. Cartoons are projected at a rate of twenty-four frames per second, so that single image of a tailless Mickey flashed by Walt's eyes in 1/24 of a second. Walt watched the entire cartoon without saying a word, and the animators thought he had missed the tailless frame. But as soon as the cartoon was over, Walt said, "It'll work—but put the tail back on Mickey before you release it."[15]

In 1937, Walt was preparing to release his first feature film, *Snow White and the Seven Dwarfs*. As he examined the footage of some of Snow White's scenes, he decided that his young heroine's cheeks were too pale. He was running out of money to reshoot the scenes—and even more critically, he was running out of time. Yet he was not content to send Snow White into the theaters with pallid cheeks. So he ordered his artists to find just the right shade of pink to give Snow White a slight blush. None of the shades they came up with satisfied Walt's eye for detail.

Finally, one of the paint artists, a young woman, dabbed some rouge from her makeup compact onto the animation cel. Walt pronounced it the perfect shade. The rouge was added to thousands of cels, the footage was reshot, and Snow White's makeover was finished just in time for her debut.

Snow White's blush was just one of thousands of details Walt personally oversaw during the production of his masterpiece. The film was a critical and commercial success. From then on, the Walt Disney Studio was no longer seen as a mere "mouse factory." Because of Walt's attention to detail, he achieved his goal of becoming one of the most respected filmmakers in the world.

Small Leaks Can Sink You

Writer John Rosevear of the *Motley Fool* has written about what he calls "annoying ways to build wealth"—little things most of us really don't want to do but that could help us achieve big financial goals. His suggestions include:

- *Skip that four-dollar Starbucks latte every morning.* He writes, "If you invest four dollars times five days a week times fifty-two weeks a year annually in an index fund returning 10 percent, you will have more than $500,000 in forty years. The math doesn't lie." Rosevear admits that you will also miss "forty years' worth of the pleasure of breaking your morning fog with a delicious beverage." Well, not necessarily. If you have a drip coffeemaker, you can home brew a cup of rich French roast coffee for about thirty cents—and for far less effort than it takes to drive to Starbucks.

- *Downsize your digs.* Do you have more room than you need? Can you get by with less? Then consider moving to a smaller house with a smaller mortgage and smaller utility payments. Then invest the savings.

- *Downsize your body.* No kidding, being overweight is expensive. Getting into shape by eating well and exercising can save you money on medical expenses, life insurance, lost work, and more.

- *Brown-bag your lunch.* In addition to being less expensive, a lunch you make yourself at home is usually healthier and lower in calories, fat, and salt. Brown bagging can be an effective way to slim your physique while fattening your wallet.

- *Buy used instead of new.* Why buy a brand-new car that loses thousands of dollars in value the moment you drive it off the lot? Let someone else take that hit, then buy the car while it still has plenty of life left in it. And, of course, you can save tons of money by buying secondhand goods at yard sales or on eBay. You might be surprised at the like-new quality you can often find at bargain-basement prices.

Rosevear concludes, "Most people react to ideas like these with a roll of the eyes. But give them a second look. One or two might make sense for you—and could help you save a lot more money over time."[16] As Benjamin Franklin so wisely observed, "Beware of little expenses. A small leak will sink a great ship."[17]

And just as small expenses can sink you, a degree or two of extra effort can vastly increase your income. Sam Parker, cofounder of GiveMore.com, observes, "At 211 degrees, water is hot. At 212 degrees, it boils. And with boiling water, comes steam. And with steam, you can power a city. One degree."[18] With just a little bit more effort, a little bit more attentiveness, a little bit more focus on the little things, we can reap exponentially greater rewards. Parker offers a number of examples.

A professional golf tournament consists of four rounds of 18 holes, one round each day for four days, a total of 72 holes. Parker notes that, over one ten-year period, the average margin of victory in all four major professional tournaments—the US Open, the British Open, the PGA Championship, and the Masters—was less than three strokes. That's less than a one-stroke difference per round. Yet the first-place winner reaped an average of 76 percent more in earnings than the second-place finisher (not counting endorsements).

Parker looked at a ten-year record of finishes at two of auto racing's top events, the Daytona 500 and the Indianapolis 500. Each race lasts longer than three hours, yet the finishes are always extremely close. Parker concludes, "In the last ten years of each race combined, the winner took the checkered flag by an average margin of 1.54 seconds and took home an average of $1,278,813 in first-place prize money. The average prize for the second-place finisher was $631,321—a difference of $647,492."[19]

What is the secret of success? There is no secret! Vast rewards usually come to those who put out a slight amount of additional effort. If your competition puts out 211 degrees of effort, then you need to expend 212 degrees. That one degree of extra effort could make all the difference in the world.

You may say, "But I'm already putting out 212 degrees of effort. There are only so many hours in a day, and I'm already going flat-out in pursuit of my goals." It's true that everybody needs rest and relaxation. We need family time. We need a little escape each day. But are you sure you couldn't squeeze just one more degree of effort out of your daily schedule? If you're like most people, bits and pieces of time are slipping through the cracks of your life. There is a technique you can use to seal up those cracks and put that time to good use. This technique might give you that extra degree of effort you need to achieve your goals—and the good news is that it couldn't be any easier.

This technique is called the Grab 15 Principle, and it was invented by nationally known time management expert Dru Scott Decker. In her book *Finding More Time in Your Life*, she observes that most people live by the "waiting-until myth." In other words, people are always waiting until they have more time, until circumstances change, until some opportunity opens up. The problem is that the long-awaited day never comes. Our schedules are always busy, and the waiting-until excuse will always be with us. Solution: the Grab 15 Principle. Here's how it works.

You have a long-cherished goal you want to achieve, a dream you want to fulfill, a project you want to complete. It might be that exercise program you want to start, that language you want to learn, or that woodworking project you've been planning. You keep saying, "Someday when I have more time, I'm going to reach for that goal." According to Decker, "someday" is now.

You can stop letting priceless, irreplaceable time slip away from you. Begin by making a commitment to grab fifteen minutes every day without fail. It doesn't matter how busy your schedule is; you can always clear fifteen minutes out of your twenty-four-hour day to invest in your dreams. Simply make a decision that your head won't hit the pillow until you have spent at least fifteen minutes working toward your goal.

Fifteen minutes is a little thing, a small amount of time. Granted, you probably won't be able to make huge strides toward your goal in a single fifteen-minute chunk of time. But you will make more progress than you would have if you hadn't committed yourself to the Grab 15 Principle. In fact, I guarantee that if you practice the Grab 15 Principle every day, you will soon discover that this principle is far more powerful than you ever imagined. Here are four reasons why:

1. *Those fifteen-minute chunks of time add up.* Let's say you take Sundays off and Grab 15 six days a week. Fifteen minutes times six days equals ninety minutes per week—or seventy-eight hours per year. Imagine what you could accomplish if someone magically added seventy-eight hours to your year. That's a lot of time—and it's time that would otherwise simply fall through the cracks of your life. With hardly any change to your busy lifestyle, you have magically added the equivalent of almost two forty-hour workweeks to your life.

2. *The Grab 15 Principle accelerates your creativity and intensifies your concentration.* This is especially important if you need a lot of mental energy to achieve your goal (for example, if you are learning a language or writing a play). The Grab 15 Principle helps you to keep thinking and meditating on your project, both consciously and subconsciously, every single day. This added reinforcement and day-to-day continuity will magnify your retention and creative energy. If you work on your goals for only a few

91

hours every few weeks, you waste a lot of time asking yourself, "Now, where was I?" The Grab 15 Principle enables you to get the most out of each fifteen-minute session.

3. *This tool, the Grab 15 Principle, imposes a daily discipline on you and keeps you energized, motivated, and working steadily toward your goal.* Once your daily fifteen-minute session becomes a habit, it quickly becomes hard to break. If you miss a day, you feel like something is wrong, and you can't wait to get back on track the following day. That's the power of a habit.

4. *Once you get going, you'll find it difficult to stop at fifteen minutes.* You'll be on a roll, and you'll want to keep going. The bonus time you put into your Grab 15 sessions will move you all the faster to your goals.[20]

Average achievers tell themselves, "I can only do a little, so I might as well do nothing." High achievers tell themselves, "Even if I can only do a little, I'm going to do as much as I can." You may not have the whole day, but you have fifteen minutes. Put those minutes to good use. They are the little things that will take you to your goals.

As the late Zig Ziglar pointed out, "I lost 37 pounds in ten months by losing 1.9 ounces per day. I wrote *See You at the Top*, a 384-page 2,000,000-copy best-seller, by writing an average of 1.26 pages every day for ten months. People who are successful at whatever they do reach their objectives by a series of little things they do every day."[21]

A 100 Percent Effort

To reach your goals in life, you must become a master of the little things, the fine details. You must make sure that small mistakes don't defeat you and set you back. And you must focus on those little positive actions you can take to give yourself an added edge, even if it's just one extra degree of advantage. Here are some principles for mastering the little things so that you can achieve your goals:

- *High performance comes from the perfection of many small and relevant details.* Sloppiness in tending to details is a common failure in mediocre individuals and organizations. The accumulation of many little things done to a high standard of performance is the key to success in high-achieving individuals and organizations.

- *If you collect enough pennies, you'll eventually be rich.* This principle is so obvious that we easily forget it, yet it holds true in basketball, business, the arts, education, the church, or any other field of endeavor. If we perfect one little thing, it probably won't make much difference. But if we perfect many little things, the cumulative effect becomes great over time. That is why a focus on the little things can lead to big results.

- *To achieve great goals, break down big, intimidating challenges into a lot of little things done well.* This principle is true whether you are trying to build a championship basketball team, write a book, or trek cross-country from enemy-held Burma to neighboring India. A journey on foot of 140 miles may seem unthinkable. That's fine. Don't think about it. Instead, think about getting to the next ridge, the next friendly village. That is how to achieve the "impossible" goals.

- *You may think you're just one little person, but one person can achieve great things.* Wangari Maathai was just one person whose "little thing" was planting trees. But she improved the lives of her people and the ecology of her planet, and she was awarded the Nobel Peace Prize. Never say, "I'm just one person." That's no excuse for doing nothing. Instead, focus on the little things, and big results will follow.

- *Every great achievement is a series of little battles.* A basketball game is a series of small skirmishes. A political campaign is a series of hundreds of speeches and rubber-chicken fund-raising dinners. A novel is a series of pages written one word, one sentence at a time. A retirement account is a series of small investments made over a period of many years. A motion picture like *Snow White and the Seven Dwarfs* is a series of tiny details lovingly embellished and projected at a rate of twenty-four frames per second. The successful achievement of any goal is always the result of a lot of little things done well.

- *Financial success is the result of a lot of little good decisions—and the wisdom to avoid a lot of little bad decisions.* Even that daily four-dollar Starbucks latte can have a big impact on your financial future. Think carefully about every little financial decision and choose wisely.

- *The secret of success is that there is no secret.* Vast rewards come to those who put out just a little extra effort, work a little bit longer, waste a little less time, and give as close to 100 percent effort as is humanly possible. No one gives a full 100 percent, but we can all focus on the little things that move us an extra percentage point closer to our full capability. Do that, and you will win far more often than you lose—and you *will* achieve your goals.

Andy Hill played for Coach Wooden from 1970 to 1972. Though Hill was at UCLA during three championship years, he was one of the few people who disliked being coached by John Wooden and left UCLA feeling embittered by his experience. Hill felt that Coach Wooden treated his players unfairly and unequally. He felt he should have gotten more playing time during those championship years.

Hill went on to a career as a successful television executive, eventually becoming president of CBS Productions. There, he had a hand in the success of such popular television series as

Dr. Quinn, Medicine Woman and *Touched by an Angel.* In that position, he had a chance to see leadership from a different vantage point. Instead of being the unhappy player sitting at the end of the bench, Hill suddenly saw things from Coach Wooden's perspective. He had to deal with impatient, unhappy, talented people with easily bruised egos. It occurred to him that most of what he knew about managing high-powered personalities involved lessons he had learned from Coach John Wooden.

One day, Hill worked up the courage to call Coach Wooden and thank him for the lessons Coach had taught him. To his surprise, Coach Wooden greeted him with enthusiasm and invited him over for a visit and conversation. After renewing his friendship with Coach Wooden, Hill wrote a book in praise of his old coach titled *Be Quick—but Don't Hurry!* In that book, he explains Coach Wooden's perspective on how to focus on the little things to achieve one's goals:

> I don't think I've ever met a more competitive man in my life [than Coach Wooden]. Coach gets genuinely annoyed when people talk about giving 110 percent effort, because the goal is ridiculous. Even giving a full 100 percent effort is only approachable, and probably never attainable. But any individual or team that gets close to a full effort will win far more than they'd lose.[22]

So focus on the little things. Focus on the little ways you can maximize your time and money, the little ways you can gain a cumulative edge, the little ways you can become more effective and more competitive. Then get ready to celebrate the achievement of your biggest goals and dreams.

5

Little Things
Produce Consistency

We were consistent. I've always believed in consistency.

Coach John Wooden

ANDRÉ MCCARTER PLAYED BASKETBALL AT UCLA from 1973 to 1976. He recalls receiving Coach Wooden's strongest "expletive" on his very first day of practice. When McCarter made one of his nifty behind-the-back bounce passes to a teammate, Coach Wooden barked, "Goodness gracious, sakes alive, André!"

Yes, that was as harsh a "cussing out" as anyone ever received from Coach Wooden. But don't let that fool you. Coach Wooden was tough, demanding, and a firm disciplinarian. He knew what he wanted from his players, and he expected them to deliver it. And one of the things he wanted most was consistency.

Though a razzle-dazzle move like a behind-the-back pass could bring the crowd to its feet, such moves were risky. When

Coach Wooden saw McCarter make that pass, he saw all the things that could go wrong—such as a loose ball or a turnover. Coach Wooden informed McCarter, "We use the basic chest pass here at UCLA."

That reprimand, mild as it was, rubbed McCarter the wrong way. McCarter and Coach Wooden were destined to knock heads. Coach had no patience for stunts and showing off. He was all business, because being all business meant consistency.

"Coach Wooden seldom raised his voice and never swore," McCarter later recalled, "but man, he could be tough. One day I was five minutes late to a pregame meal. The next four games I lost my place in the starting lineup."

The big showdown came at the first practice of McCarter's sophomore year. Coach Wooden blew his whistle, and the practice game began. The ball was inbounded to the starting point guard, whose job McCarter wanted. McCarter made a quick move, stole the ball, and flew down court. All McCarter had to do was pass the ball to one of his wide-open teammates for an easy layup. But that wasn't McCarter's style. Instead, he faked a behind-the-back pass, kept the ball, and drained it himself, leaving star center Bill Walton flat-footed. It was a brilliant demonstration of showmanship.

But Coach Wooden was livid. "Goodness gracious, sakes alive, André," he shouted. "You do that again and you won't play on our team!"

McCarter's stunt play and Coach Wooden's angry reaction set the stage for the next few weeks of their rocky relationship. McCarter wanted to show off his skills. Coach Wooden demanded fundamentals and consistency.

When a coach from a rival school offered McCarter the freedom to play his flamboyant style of basketball, McCarter seriously considered leaving UCLA. He phoned his mother and said, "Coach and I aren't getting along. I'm thinking of leaving."

His mother replied, "It sounds to me like you're not thinking, period. Coach Wooden won a whole bunch of championships before you got there. He must know something you haven't figured out yet."

For days, McCarter considered his mother's words. Finally, he prayed, "Lord, give me the strength to put my ego aside. Help me change my attitude."

McCarter felt God prompting him to learn everything he could about Coach Wooden. So he went to the library and looked up every article Coach had written or that had been written about him. He studied Coach Wooden's basketball philosophy and belief system, especially his famed Pyramid of Success. McCarter was especially impressed with the cornerstones of the Pyramid, industriousness, cooperation, and enthusiasm.

A few days later, Coach Wooden talked to the team about consistency. "Winning basketball," he said, "has nothing to do with the highlight plays you see on television. Teams win because they play unselfishly, and their players have solid fundamentals." As McCarter listened to Coach speak, everything clicked into place. He realized that Coach Wooden was not just preparing them to play basketball. "Basketball," McCarter concluded, "was just something to prepare us to be good students of life."

As a result of his new understanding of Coach Wooden, McCarter completely changed his attitude and his style of play. Instead of driving selfishly to the basket, he made unspectacular but consistently reliable chest passes to his waiting teammates. In McCarter's junior year, Coach Wooden made him the starting point guard and urged him to become a leader on the court. After the Bruins beat Kentucky to win the national championship—Coach Wooden's tenth—Coach told McCarter, "You were my coach on the floor."

It was the best compliment McCarter could have received, and it was all he could do to keep from crying on the spot. He would have cried if he had known that Coach Wooden had just coached the last season of his career. Coach retired after that championship.

McCarter learned a lesson that served him well not only in basketball but also in life. A razzle-dazzle behind-the-back pass may be a crowd-pleaser, but it's the fundamentals, the little things, that make a consistent winner. That was the message Coach Wooden was trying to get across to young McCarter, and years later, McCarter is glad his coach got through to him.[1]

The Consistency of French Fries

Consistency was always very important to Coach Wooden. In *Wooden on Leadership*, he wrote:

> I am very leery of excess in most things—language, dress, hair cuts, and much else. But I especially dislike emotional excess because it produces inconsistency. . . . The hallmark of successful leadership is consistently maximum performance. Emotionalism opens a leader to inconsistency. Seek intensity coupled with emotional discipline. Display those behaviors and then demand them from those you lead. A leader with a volatile temperament is vulnerable. And so is the team he or she leads.[2]

One of the most intense rivalries in the NFL is between the New England Patriots and the Indianapolis Colts. Tony Dungy, who coached the Colts from 2002 until his retirement in 2008, wrote about one key game in that rivalry, a Monday night duel in Massachusetts on November 7, 2005, against the defending Super Bowl champion Patriots. Though the Colts were undefeated (7–0) thus far, the Colts' quarterback, Peyton Manning, was winless (0–7) against New England in Foxboro. Going into that game, Dungy knew the key to winning was consistency.

"I kept preaching to our guys," Dungy recalled, "that we shouldn't think about it being New England. We just needed to focus on the Colts. We needed to think about what it took for us to play well and not worry about anything else."

The team got the message. Manning kept the Patriots defense on their heels all night, finishing the game with a record 28 out of 37 completions for 321 yards and three touchdowns. Running back Edgerrin James gained 104 yards on 34 carries. Receivers Marvin Harrison and Reggie Wayne both had 100-yard receiving games.

"We won, 40–21," Dungy wrote. Now the Colts were 8–0, but Coach Dungy knew there was a danger in that victory over New England. "I started to get concerned about how the media would react to this win. After [we had beaten] the defending champs in their stadium, I was sure [the media] would be ready to anoint us the new kings. . . . I wanted to make sure we didn't fall into that trap."

After the game, Coach Dungy stood before the team and delivered a talk designed to put that victory into perspective. He began with a verse from Scripture, Proverbs 16:18: "Pride goes before destruction, a haughty spirit before a fall." Then he told his team, "We won big today, but let's not forget how we did it. We worked hard. This was only one game, and now it's over. We need to continue to do what we do."

In other words, the Indianapolis Colts needed to be consistent. They couldn't afford to be one team against the Super Bowl champion Patriots one week and a different team against the 0-7 Houston Texans the following week. Coach Dungy worried that all the adulation in the press would give them prideful egos and a haughty spirit—which would lead to a fall. As he stood before his team, groping for a way to illustrate the point he wanted to get across to them, he thought about his children and one of their favorite things when they were growing up: McDonald's french fries.

Dungy told his players:

> The beauty of McDonald's is that they are consistent. The reason my kids like McDonald's is that they always know what they're going to get. It's not gourmet food, but the french fries they order in Indianapolis are just like the french fries they order in Tampa. Wherever they get McDonald's fries, they know it will be the same. That's what McDonald's does. They don't make french fries in New England more special than the ones they make in Houston. We have to do the same. We can't view any game as more important than another. Just like McDonald's, we need to keep making the same good fries.

Coach Dungy's french fries analogy got the point across. The following week, his Colts produced the same consistently good product in Indianapolis against the Texans that they had produced in Foxboro. Manning's stats were hauntingly similar to his stats in Foxboro. He completed 26 out of 35 passes for 297 yards and three touchdowns. Edgerrin James and Marvin Harrison again had 100-yard games. Their performance could not have been more consistent. That game—a 31–17 victory over the Texans—was indeed the McDonald's french fries of football games.[3]

Truett Cathy, founder of the Atlanta-based Chick-fil-A fast-food chain, says that consistency is one of the keys to his company's success, and his company maintains consistency by paying attention to the little things. In his book *Eat Mor Chikin: Inspire More People*, he writes:

> I have always looked for better ways to do things, and when I learned about a truly automated coffee machine, I had to see it in operation. The company that supplied our equipment, Whitlock Dobbs Inc., arranged a demonstration.

Commercial coffee makers in those days resembled the home brewing equipment that we use today. You put in a filter and coffee, and the machine sprayed water through. Then you took the bag out of the top, dumped out the grounds, and started over again. Every pot tasted a little different because everybody put in a slightly different amount of coffee.

But with this new coffee maker, I can put coffee in a bin, hook the machine up to the water supply, and it did the rest. All I had to do was push buttons, and it measured the coffee and water, made the coffee, dumped the grounds, and washed itself. I bought the first one in the Atlanta area, and our customers became the first in town to enjoy the most consistent cup of coffee around.

Consistency, I had learned, is important in the restaurant business. Customers don't like surprises. If they have a good experience, they want to repeat that experience—all the way down to the coffee.[4]

Paul Buyer is a professor of music and director of percussion at Clemson University. He is also a motivational speaker and the author of *Working toward Excellence*. In that book, Buyer writes, "Consistency refers to repeatedly doing the things that will put you in a position to succeed. When inconsistency occurs, 'count-ability' suffers, which is your ability to count on someone or something to deliver what you expect. Be careful not to underestimate the value of consistency when working toward excellence. As the great philosopher Aristotle said, 'We are what we repeatedly do. Excellence, then, is not an act, but a habit.'"[5]

I once got a call from an editor at *Reader's Digest*. They wanted to run a quote of mine in an upcoming edition. I had been quoted in a newspaper talking about Stanley Roberts, a big, heavy center who used to play for the Magic. I had said, "Our team doctor told Stanley to eat from the seven basic food groups, but when Stanley was finished eating, there were only five food groups left."

The editor said, "I checked with the Food Administration in Washington, DC, and they inform me that there are only five basic food groups, not seven. We need to change your quote." Well, there *had* been seven basic food groups when I was growing up, but apparently the government had misplaced a couple of food groups along the way.

I said, "Fine, use the joke and change the numbers—when Stanley was finished eating, there were only three food groups left. By the way, do you fact-check everything that goes into *Reader's Digest*, even the jokes?"

"We sure do," he said. "We have a whole staff that checks out the accuracy of everything we print, every detail."

That is an excellent example of what it means to pay attention to the little things. That intense attention to detail enables *Reader's Digest* to maintain consistency and quality, issue after issue, year after year.

Billy Graham's daughter Ruth is the author of a number of books, including *A Legacy of Faith: Things I Learned from My Father*. In that book, she made this remarkable observation about her father, the world-famous evangelist:

> Over his lifetime my father has remained remarkably consistent in his focus on evangelism, consistent in his mission—another mark of the authentic life. You pick up his preoccupation in his conversation; he always pulls talk around to God. If he makes an appearance on a talk show, regardless of the questions, he finds a way to turn conversation back to the gospel. . . . Daddy doesn't waver. . . . He focuses on God, and personal faith in Christ, whenever and wherever he can.[6]

Former General Electric CEO Jack Welch preaches consistency as an essential component of success in business.

> You don't get anywhere if you keep changing your ideas. The only way to change people's minds is with consistency. Once

you get ideas, you keep refining them and improving them. The more simply your idea is defined, the better it is. You communicate, you communicate, and then you communicate some more. Consistency, simplicity, and repetition [are] what it's all about.[7]

Successful people in every field of endeavor will tell you that if you want to be successful, you must be consistent. And as Coach Wooden always taught his players, you must be consistent in the little things.

Little Things That Produce Consistent Results

Whether you are a business leader, a leader in some other field of endeavor, or an employee who dreams of being a leader someday, there are some specific little things you can do to become consistently effective in your life and career. Let me offer ten suggestions:

1. *Consistently think of others.* You already know what's important to you. To be consistently successful, you have to continually think of what is important to others. If you are a business leader, think about what your customers and clients want and need. If you are a religious leader, try to put yourself in the place of the people in your congregation. If you are an employee, try to imagine the pressures and problems of your boss, then figure out ways to make yourself more valuable to the organization. What problems can you solve for others? How can you add value to the lives of others? How can you make yourself indispensable to other people? If you consistently focus on others, you will become more consistently successful.

2. *Consistently speak the language other people understand.* Businesspeople, educators, government workers, people in the sports world, pastors, and people in other segments of society tend to develop their own language, their own

jargon, their own abbreviations and shorthand terms. That's fine as long as you're speaking to other people in your own little culture and they understand such terms as *orthogonal*, *problematize*, *mimetic isomorphism*, and *computationally intensive content analysis*. But when you step outside your professional clique, you need to speak the language of everyday people. Author and television correspondent Polly LaBarre has correctly labeled technically confusing speech "jargon monoxide," a deadly verbal poison that asphyxiates communication.[8] For consistent success, communicate in everyday language.

3. *Be consistently prompt.* Show up at appointments on time—or better yet, ten minutes early. Return emails and phone calls promptly. When your customers, clients, or employer inform you of a problem you need to solve, solve it promptly, then promptly report that you've taken care of it. Build a reputation as someone who gets things done—promptly and consistently.

4. *Consistently deliver more than is expected.* Don't just satisfy your customers, wow them. Don't just meet your boss's expectations, amaze her. Come in earlier, stay later, work harder, produce more, produce higher quality, offer more value, attract more clients, and generate more glowing reviews than anyone expected. Offer freebies, unexpected gifts, extra value, and over-the-top effort. Deliver more and charge less. If you run a company by delivering more than is expected, your customers will become your most effective marketers and salespeople. If you are an employee and you deliver more than is expected, your boss will become your biggest booster. Show the people you serve that they come first, that you value them, that you are loyal to them, that you care about them and you will experience rising success on a steady, consistent basis.

5. *Consistently follow up with people.* When your boss or your customer does something nice for you, show your

appreciation. Follow up with a small gift or a thank-you note (handwritten, not an email!). People appreciate these little demonstrations of thoughtfulness far more than you know. These are just little things, but if you make a human connection by following up with people, they will reward you with their loyalty.

6. *Consistently make people feel special.* Never let up, never slack off, never take people for granted. Call people by name. Ask for their opinions. Keep every promise. Treat every customer or client as an honored guest, whether it's their first visit or their hundred and first. Make them feel like they are insiders, VIPs, your best friend forever. Show them you care—not just about their business or what they can do for you. Show them you care about *them* and their needs.

7. *Consistently be kind to people's children.* If you have a business oriented toward grown-ups, be aware that grown-ups sometimes bring their kids in tow. Keep a stack of coloring books and crayons under the counter (imprinted with the company logo—that's a nice touch!) for those times when kids get restless or bored. When you show you care about the happiness of people's kids, you immediately connect with those parents at the heart level. Showing consideration for people's children is such a little thing, but it can have a huge impact.

8. *Be consistently, personally present.* This is a principle I learned from one of my mentors, the great baseball promoter Bill Veeck. After every game, he would stand at the gate of his ballpark and personally thank people for coming to the games. I began following his example from my earliest days as a minor league baseball general manager, and I still practice that policy to this day. Don't just put up a sign that says, "Thank you for your business." Stand at the door, greet people as they come in, thank them as they go out, and make them feel welcomed and appreciated at all times.

9. *Deliver consistent quality.* Whatever business you're in, whether you are the boss or an employee, make sure you consistently deliver the McDonald's french fries of your profession. Whether you are trying to please a boss or a customer, that person wants to know he or she can expect a consistently high level of quality from you, time after time after time. Never disappoint. Never lower your standards. Always maintain the same high standard of quality. Consistency is the key to your success.

10. *Maintain your consistent integrity.* Never cut an ethical corner just to make a little extra profit. Never lie to an employer, employee, or customer. If you make a mistake, admit it. People think much more highly of those who admit errors and apologize than those who engage in cover-ups and evasions. Always practice the Golden Rule: treat your employer, your employees, and your customers as you would have them treat you.

Consistent Effort Yields Predictable Success

British mystery writer Alex Keegan is the author of numerous novels and short stories. His books include *Cuckoo*, *Razorbill*, and *A Wild Justice*. Keegan made a careful study of rejection and came to an interesting conclusion: If a writer maintains a consistent attack of the publishing markets, he or she will tend to develop a consistent and predictable ratio of sales versus rejections. "It's a fact," says Keegan, "that the more you submit, the more you will be rejected, but . . . [you] cannot fail if you work at your art, if you read, read, read, write, write, write, submit, submit, submit."

To prove his thesis, Keegan started a "boot camp" of committed but largely unpublished fiction writers. There were eleven founding members of the boot camp, eight of whom had no publishing credits at all. The rules for membership in the group were tough and demanding. Each writer in the group had to produce one short story every two weeks. The group would critique it, then the writer would revise it and submit it for publication.

During the first year of the group, those eleven writers amassed an impressive number of professional sales—eighty-five stories sold for publication in print, online, or broadcast venues. One member of the group won the BBC World Service's Short Story of the Year award. Keegan himself sold a novel and forty short pieces that year.

The group was so successful that they stayed together for another year—and the group racked up two hundred sales. The year after that, three hundred fifty sales. The reason for the increased sales, of course, was increased submissions. But more submissions also meant more rejections. That first year, Keegan said, "I had more rejections than in the previous forty-nine years of my life. But rejections are side effects, meaningless. . . . I kept my belief in myself, my work."

Using a spreadsheet, Keegan charted his submissions and was able to calculate a "hit rate"—a ratio of sales per submissions. He found that by consistently submitting story after story, he had developed a consistent hit rate of one sale for every 3.5 submissions. As a result, Keegan learned to view rejections not as failures but as feedback. Because he had developed a consistent "batting average," every rejection slip just brought him one step closer to his next sale.

"I can count," Keegan concluded. "I know that three rejections mean a sale. I welcome rejections. . . . I eat rejections like Popeye eats spinach."[9]

The moral to this story is that consistent effort yields predictable success. Whether you are a writer like Alex Keegan, a salesman trying to make a living on commissions, an entrepreneur launching a new product, or an employee hoping to rise quickly in an organization, the key to success is consistency in the little things. If you do a lot of little things well, and do them again and again at the same consistent level over a long period of time, you *will* succeed. Here are some principles for becoming consistent in the little things so that you can achieve your goals:

- *Consistency may not be flashy, but consistency produces success.* And success is the best razzle-dazzle play of all. After all, would you rather dazzle a crowd with a behind-the-back pass or rack up a string of national championships? Once André McCarter got his priorities straight and his ego in check, he was able to appreciate Coach Wooden's philosophy of consistency.

- *Consistency means never letting down, never slacking off.* Winners don't treat one game, one product, one act of service as more special than another. Winners put forth a consistently high level of effort every single time—no exceptions.

- *Customers don't like surprises, so give them a good repeat experience, again and again and again.* Whether you are making cups of coffee, bags of french fries, novels, sermons, automobiles, or any other product, make sure you meet or exceed expectations time after time. A single disappointing customer experience could send that customer straight to your competitor—forever.

- *Consistency in the little things requires you to empathize with others.* You can't be successful by focusing only on your own wants, needs, and tastes. You must develop the ability to put yourself in the shoes and mind-set of your boss or your customers. You must find ways to make yourself and your product or service indispensable to others.

- *Consistently show you care.* Promptly return calls, send thank-you notes, demonstrate thoughtfulness, and make people feel welcomed and appreciated, time after time.

- *Maintain consistent character.* Never cut ethical corners. Never lie. Own up to mistakes. Treat everyone as you would like to be treated.

- *Consistent effort yields predictable success.* Don't give up. Keep making a consistent effort. Don't let rejection, failure, or disappointment stop you. Believe in yourself. You will succeed if you maintain consistency in the little things.

After André McCarter left UCLA, he went on to play two seasons in the NBA, then went into coaching at Haverford College in Pennsylvania. From there he returned to UCLA, where he served as an assistant coach under another John Wooden protégé, Walt Hazzard. Hazzard had played on Coach Wooden's first championship team in 1964.

Years passed. One day, McCarter wondered, *Have I ever properly thanked Coach Wooden for his impact on my life?* While McCarter and his wife were watching a White House awards ceremony on a television news show, his wife asked him, "Why don't you nominate Coach for a Presidential Medal of Freedom?"

So McCarter researched the award, which had been established by President Harry Truman in 1945 as a way of recognizing distinguished civilian service in peacetime. Then McCarter collected more than thirty letters of recommendation from people who knew Coach Wooden, and he submitted Coach Wooden's name to the Clinton administration. Nothing happened. In 2001, McCarter resubmitted Coach's name to the George W. Bush administration. Still nothing happened. In 2002, he submitted Coach's name again.

Though no reply came from the White House, McCarter was surprised and pleased to read an article in the *Los Angeles Times* announcing that Coach John Wooden would receive the nation's highest civilian honor, the Presidential Medal of Freedom.

Not long afterward, McCarter met with Coach Wooden and, though choked with tears, managed to tell his old coach how much he loved him and how he continued to apply the lessons Coach Wooden had taught him. McCarter had learned the lessons Coach Wooden had tried so hard to teach him, including the lesson of showing gratitude.

"We had come full circle," McCarter concluded.[10]

To be successful, be consistent. To be consistent, pay close attention to the little things.

6

Little Things Lead to Excellence

If you don't have time to do it right, when will you have time to do it over?

Coach John Wooden

ONE OF COACH WOODEN'S CHIEF CONCERNS AS a teacher and coach at UCLA was excellence. He wanted to raise up a cadre of scholar-athletes—well-rounded, well-balanced individuals who would excel both on and off the court. UCLA was not a school where professors would give athletes a special dispensation. A Bruins athlete was expected to demonstrate both brainpower and athletic prowess—and believe it or not, brainpower came first.

Asked about his recruiting process, Coach Wooden replied, "The first thing we wanted to find out was whether he had the grades to get in. The next thing I would want to find out would be how quick he is in relation to others in the position he would be playing in college. I consider quickness to be the most important physical asset of an athlete. Second to quickness I want to know what kind of person he was; was he a team player?"[1]

A 1961 study of all male sophomores, juniors, and seniors at UCLA revealed a grade point average of 2.49. At that time, Coach Wooden's players averaged just under that figure, 2.33. This is a remarkable accomplishment, especially for such an academically demanding school as UCLA.

Year after year, Coach Wooden distributed a handout to all his Bruins basketball players, and the handout stressed both academic excellence and excellence in character:

1. You are in school for an education. Keep that first in your thoughts, but play basketball second.
2. Do not cut classes and do be on time.
3. Do not fall behind and do get your work in on time.
4. Have regular study hours and keep them.
5. Arrange with your professors in advance when you must be absent.
6. Do not expect favors. Do your part.
7. Arrange for tutoring at the first sign of trouble.
8. Work for a high grade point average. Do not be satisfied by merely meeting the eligibility requirements.
9. Do your assignments to the best of your ability, but never be too proud to seek help and advice.
10. Earn the respect of everyone.[2]

Coach John Wooden produced such a high level of excellence in his basketball program that the Bruins became known as a near-invincible opponent. UCLA was so dominant that many sportswriters and rival coaches openly questioned whether Coach Wooden's program was good for college basketball.

One sportswriter complained, "What John Wooden has done in college basketball is to wreck it." Another moaned, "Gets rather monotonous, doesn't it? UCLA week after week, month after month, season after season, winning every basketball game it plays." And yet another griped, "It's a sad thing what has happened to college basketball. UCLA makes everybody else play for second place."

Nothing but sour grapes. It wasn't as if Coach Wooden had built his team by cheating. In fact, he had drilled an exceptionally high degree of character and integrity into his players. He demanded scholarship first, athletics second. All these complaints were simply complaints about the extremely high level of excellence Coach Wooden had achieved through his players.

Coach let these small-minded complaints roll right off his back. "Rather than calling what we have achieved a dynasty," he said, "I prefer to think of it as a cycle. And I believe all cycles come to an end. But certain things can make the cycle extend longer than normal. Little things, such as attentiveness to detail. Things that don't show up in the box scores. Things that help a player shoot better, rebound better, switch men on defense better. They're only minor things but they mean a great deal."[3]

If anyone cared to listen, Coach Wooden was announcing the secret of his success, the secret of UCLA basketball's dominance during the 1960s. He was telling other coaches, in effect, "If you want to achieve what we have achieved at UCLA, then simply do what we are doing at UCLA. Focus on the little things that lead to excellence. Pay attention to the details that give you that slight edge over your competition. The reason UCLA excels can be found in all these little things we do. If you do them in your program, you will excel too."

And, of course, what is true in basketball is true in every other endeavor in life. Coach Wooden believed that no one should ever settle for mediocrity but should continually strive for excellence. "Being average," he once observed, "means you are as close to the bottom as you are to the top."[4] Excellence is a matter of being attentive to detail. If you want to excel in business, the military, academia, sports, government, or any other field, then you must major in the little things that lead to excellence.

Little Actions, Revolutionary Results

Julie Fenster, author of *In the Words of Great Business Leaders*, writes about John D. Rockefeller, the founder of Standard Oil Company, who was the first American billionaire and is regarded as the richest person in history, after adjusting for inflation. Fenster writes:

> Stories of Rockefeller's attention to detail were legendary. As president of the new concern, every single penny was of interest to him. It was a question of business practice. A penny was the stuff of his life, the stuff of business: It could not be inconsequential. Once he asked a workman soldering the tops of metal barrels how many dots of solder were used. Forty, he was told. "Have you tried thirty-eight?" Rockefeller asked. As it turned out, thirty-eight dots of solder made a seal that leaked. However, thirty-nine worked. In other cases, Rockefeller sent memos to low-ranking clerks pointing out minute errors he'd detected in his own perusal of company records. But no detail was minute.[5]

Rockefeller once described his own view of the little things in these words: "Of detail work I feel I have done my full share. As I began my business life as a bookkeeper, I learned to have great respect for figures and facts, no matter how small they were. . . . I had a passion for detail which afterward I was forced to strive to modify."[6] I'm convinced it was Rockefeller's self-described "passion for detail" that contributed greatly to making him the richest man who ever lived.

Yap Kim Wah served in various executive positions over a thirty-five-year period with Singapore Airlines. He once gave an interview to *Fast Company* in which he talked about attention to the little things as one of the keys to the company's success. He said:

> The most important thing that you can do for customers is to make them feel cared for as individuals. That means doing the little things, looking for opportunities to provide extra customer care. It means making passengers feel as if everything you do were especially for them. . . .
>
> On a recent overseas flight, one of our attendants noticed a toddler who kept dropping his pacifier. Every time he dropped it, he would cry, and either his mother or another passenger would retrieve the pacifier, or the flight attendant would get it as she walked by. Finally, the attendant picked up the pacifier, attached it to a ribbon, and sewed it to the child's shirt. The child was happy, the mother was happy, and the passengers nearby gave the attendant a standing ovation for solving the problem so cleverly.
>
> That kind of personal attention makes all the difference in the world.[7]

Business writer and leadership consultant Lisa Earle McLeod recalls an experience she and her family had when they moved her college-age daughter to the campus of Boston University. The four of them—mother, father, college daughter, and younger sister—were looking at a campus map, trying to figure out where to go. An official-looking man approached and asked, "Can I help you find something?"

It turned out that this man, Dean Kenneth Elmore, was the dean of students. He had offered to help not merely because he was friendly and outgoing but because helping people was official Boston University campus policy. The university has a rule for all staff members: if you see someone looking at one of the campus maps, you are to approach that person and offer help.

This policy may seem like a little thing, but Elmore said that the university sees it as an opportunity to demonstrate the values and philosophy of the university. Boston University's stated purpose is to educate students "to be reflective, resourceful individuals ready to live, adapt, and lead in an interconnected world." If we truly believe we are interconnected, then we should take the time to help each other.

Elmore added that if he sees a staff member walk past people at the campus map, he goes to that staff member and says, "We need to have a conversation and think about whether or not you should still work here." That's how important Boston University considers the "little thing" of reaching out to help people on campus. Elmore concludes, "Our goal is to be helpful. We care about people, and we place a high priority on interpersonal interactions."[8]

What starts as a rule quickly becomes a self-reinforcing part of the organizational culture. As staff members become intentionally aware of the people around them, personal outreach and caring begin to spread in other ways. For example, the grounds have become cleaner because increasingly observant staff members have begun picking up litter around the campus.

Lisa Earle McLeod suggests that every organization should adopt one little thing, one seemingly small but pivotal behavior, that symbolizes the organization's values and purpose. It should be an action that takes less than a minute to perform, something that anyone and everyone in the organization can easily do, something that everyone can hold others accountable for, and something for which there are no excuses for not doing it. Let this one little action symbolize the new attitude you want everyone in your organization to demonstrate. Then watch how that one little action revolutionizes your entire organization.[9]

Harriet Beecher Stowe, the abolitionist author whose antislavery novel *Uncle Tom's Cabin* helped ignite the Civil War and end slavery in America, once observed, "To be really great in little things, to be truly noble and heroic in the insipid details of everyday life, is a virtue so rare as to be worthy of canonization."[10]

No Little Jobs

Librettist and theatrical producer Oscar Hammerstein II once remarked on an aerial photo of the Statue of Liberty taken from a helicopter. He described how the photo revealed finely etched strands of hair atop the head of Lady Liberty, details placed there by sculptor Frédéric-Auguste Bartholdi. It's important to remember that the Statue of Liberty was dedicated in New York Harbor on October 28, 1886, almost two decades before the Wright brothers' first flight. In those days, no one believed that human beings would ever be able to fly over the statue and look down on the top of Lady Liberty's head. Yet Bartholdi refused to cut corners with his sculpture. He paid attention to the little things, to the fine details he thought no one would ever see.

Hammerstein concluded, "When you are creating a work of art, or any other kind of work, finish the job off perfectly. You never know when a helicopter, or some other instrument not at the moment invented, may come along and find you out."[11] It's true. These little things, these tiny details that we think no one will ever notice, are often the very details that spell the difference between success and failure.

Business writer Joseph Michelli tells a couple of stories that illustrate how attention to the little things distinguishes the high level of service at the Ritz-Carlton luxury hotel company. For example, there is the story of Emnet Andu, a restaurant server at the downtown Atlanta Ritz-Carlton. Andu explains:

A lady . . . asked for grape jelly. Unfortunately, we had only strawberry and raspberry. I let her know the options that were available, and told her I would do everything in my power to get her the grape jelly she desired. I then went back to my team and let them know I needed to go to the nearby store to purchase grape jelly, and they gladly provided me coverage and support. You should have seen the lady's face when I returned with the jelly. She asked where I got it, and I answered her. In that moment, the lady knew that I viewed her as important to me. . . . I know it's a little thing but it always seems to be the little things that build lifetime relationships with guests.[12]

The second story is told by Daniel Mangione, a former pastry sous chef at the Ritz-Carlton in Sarasota, Florida. One day, he received a call from a woman in the community, asking if he could recommend a bakery. The woman's daughter would soon be turning eight years old, and because of the girl's allergy to soy products, the woman was looking for a bakery that would produce a soy-free cake. She had called bakery after bakery and was repeatedly told, "We have no time or interest in researching the ingredients for your special order."

Mangione wasn't sure why the woman had called the Ritz-Carlton for a referral to a helpful bakery, but—true to the culture and values of the Ritz-Carlton organization—he made up his mind to provide this woman and her daughter the help they needed. He told the woman, "Ma'am, I am more than happy to create a birthday cake without using soy products." He reviewed with her the ingredients for the cake, then he made the cake, decorated it with frosting and candles, and had it ready on the day of the party.

The following day, the woman returned and asked to speak to Mangione. She was in tears. At first, the chef was worried that her daughter had experienced a bad reaction to the cake. But no, the woman wept tears of joy because her daughter's birthday party had gone perfectly, thanks to Mangione's thoughtfulness and extra effort.

The woman was not even a guest at the hotel, but it's not hard to imagine the loyalty and word-of-mouth advertising that this act of kindness brought to the Ritz-Carlton organization for years to come. Reflecting on the culture of the organization, Mangione concluded, "Where else would I be allowed to do something like that?"[13]

These are the little things that add up to a big reputation for excellence and first-class customer care. These are the little things that spell the difference between a good organization and a great organization. Great organizations such as the Ritz-Carlton trust and empower their people to do all the little things that make a big difference in their customers' experience.

Great leaders are people who take great interest in the little things. Business author Shawn Graham (*Courting Your Career: Match Yourself with the Perfect Job*) recalls one of his favorite bosses, a regional manager at a home improvement chain. Graham writes that this manager

> repeatedly taught us the importance of noticing the little things (his enthusiasm for details often putting him at risk of an aneurism). He made sure we checked for everything from burned-out light bulbs to guaranteeing that we always had the right items in stock. Everything we do is about brand . . . our personal brand, our office brand, our company brand. Customers and clients will notice empty handout racks, not returning phone calls within twenty-four hours, and cigarette butts on the sidewalk.[14]

Graham recalls another favorite boss who noticed the little things about her employees—the little signs and nonverbal cues that suggested an employee was feeling stressed and pressured. She had a cure for stress that never failed: Silly Putty. When this boss joined the organization, she could see that the entire staff was experiencing a lot of stress. So at the weekly staff meeting, she passed out Silly Putty to all the participants. Almost instantly, Graham could sense the entire group becoming more relaxed. The stress in the room seemed to evaporate. Graham learned an important lesson from his boss and her Silly Putty cure: "Always keep your eyes open to see if your co-workers are struggling. Some people will ask for help, others won't. Being able to pick up on the non-verbal cues that the team is under pressure is a must."[15]

Don Soderquist joined Walmart as executive vice president in 1980. He worked alongside founder Sam Walton in a number of key executive roles. Following Sam Walton's death in 1992, Don became the "keeper of the culture" of Walmart. On a single day in August 1980, the Walmart corporation opened three stores in Huntsville, Alabama. At one store, Soderquist and Walton took part in a ribbon-cutting ceremony. The moment the ribbon was cut, customers flooded through the doors, clogging the aisles.

Soderquist wrote about that day, recalling, "Sam jumped in and began to bag merchandise. He handed out candy to the kids and did anything he could think of to help the customers." Walton also used the store's public address system to thank his customers and apologize for the delays and long lines. He offered to personally assist any customer who needed help finding products in the store.

That store opening was a revelation for Soderquist. He had always considered himself one of the most service-oriented executives in the world, but when he saw Walton in action, Soderquist realized he had a thing or two to learn from his new boss. "Sam taught me a valuable lesson that day," Soderquist reflected. "None of us are too good to do the little jobs. In fact, there are no little jobs. If the chairman of the board wasn't too high and mighty to hand out lollipops and bag goods—neither was I."[16]

As veteran broadcaster and author Art Linkletter once wisely said, "Do a little more than you're paid to. Give a little more than you have to. Try a little harder than you want to. Aim a little higher than you think possible."[17] Focus on the little things, the little demonstrations of extra effort, and you will achieve excellence, guaranteed.

The Relentless Pursuit of Excellence

Anyone can focus on the big things, but true excellence is always a matter of a lot of little things done well. Here are some key principles to remember as you pursue excellence throughout your life and your career:

- *Excellence may be cyclical, but you can extend each cycle through careful attention to the little things.* The details that produce excellent performances and winning records are so seemingly minor that many people miss them altogether. Yet these little things actually give you a competitive edge and separate the merely good individuals, organizations, and teams from the truly great ones.

- *Attention to small details can give you or your organization a reputation for excellence.* A Singapore Airlines flight attendant sewed a pacifier to a child's shirt and pleased not only the mother but also many other passengers. A Boston University dean of students stopped to help a family one day, and now his entire university is receiving praise in this book. And the same is true of a restaurant server and a sous chef for the Ritz-Carlton. If you want to build a reputation for quality, start with the little things.

- *Excellence is often a matter of surprising people with small acts of unexpected grace and courtesy.* Going a little out of your way to provide some grape jelly or a special-order birthday cake can make a huge, lasting impression of excellence. That kind of caring brings tears to a customer's eyes. It makes you and your organization unforgettable.

- *Excellence may be simply a matter of noticing when people are stressed and giving them a moment of relief.* Shawn Graham will never forget the boss who handed out Silly Putty to her overstressed workers. You can probably think of a boss, a pastor, or a teacher who knew when you had reached your breaking point and knew exactly what to say to talk you down from the ledge. It doesn't necessarily take a big effort to make people feel better. Usually, it's a matter of the little things people do and say.

- *Excellence is often a matter of realizing that there are no little jobs.* Great leaders do whatever needs to be done, even bagging merchandise and handing out candy to children. If you truly strive for excellence, be willing to do all the little things that need to be done.

Denny Crum, former head basketball coach at the University of Louisville, played for Coach Wooden and was later mentored by him as a UCLA assistant coach. Crum recalls, "In the fall of 1956, I was a junior transfer preparing for my first practice. I got dressed, taped and arrived at the court early. To my surprise, Coach Wooden was already there, using a broom and wet towel to sweep the floor. Here was a successful coach of a major college basketball program, and all I could think of was, *Wow! This guy is mopping the floor?*"[18]

Coach John Wooden didn't consider himself too important to do the "little jobs." It was an unorthodox way to run a basketball program. But then, Coach Wooden didn't pursue orthodoxy. He pursued excellence.

In almost every aspect of the game of basketball, Coach Wooden operated by a different approach than most other coaches. Take rebounding, for example. At that time, most college coaches taught their players to put both hands above their head to better snatch the rebound out of the air. Not Coach Wooden. When his players went for a rebound, he had them hold their hands shoulder-high, *not* above their heads. Coach believed that the ball often rebounded at a lower angle, below shoulder level, so a player with his hands held high was actually at a disadvantage.

"A small thing, perhaps," Coach Wooden said, "but over the years I observed it made a difference in performance results. UCLA players often were able to out-rebound taller opponents."[19]

Coach Wooden also had a different approach than most coaches when it came to drilling his players on free throws. Many college basketball coaches would routinely have their players shoot as many as a hundred free throws at each practice. The theory, of course, is that practice makes perfect. But Coach Wooden didn't accept that theory. He didn't want his players to go through the motion of throwing basketballs at backboards and calling it practice. He wanted his players to become *excellent* at free throws.

So at the end of every practice session, he would have his players shoot free throws until they had completed ten successful free throws in a row. If a player could shoot ten for ten, he was done. With this approach, Coach Wooden put the emphasis on excellence, not merely on activity. He focused his players' minds on consistent, dependable, excellent results, and his players' free throw shooting contributed to Coach Wooden's amazing record.

Another way Coach Wooden differed from most of his colleagues was that he was extremely flexible in his approach to individual players and very careful not to overcoach. Some players would come into his program with nonstandard ways of doing things. Many coaches would have told those players, "You're doing it all wrong. Here's the right way to do it."

Coach Wooden, however, would actually allow some players to do things the "wrong" way as long as it was working for them. He knew that trying to get a player to alter his technique would sometimes ruin that player's game. So Coach Wooden would always observe a player for a while before coaching him and trying to change him.

One example was Keith Wilkes, who, under the name Jamaal Wilkes, went on to a long and successful NBA career. Coach Wooden was flabbergasted when he saw Wilkes shoot free throws. Wilkes would line up to shoot and actually raise the ball behind his head before launching the shot. "You could hardly make it any more difficult on yourself," Coach observed, "unless you were blindfolded." But the problem with Wilkes was that he rarely missed. In spite of his crazy technique, he hit 87.2 percent of his free throws during his first season with the Bruins. When a player's unorthodox style worked best, Coach didn't change it. As he once said, "An effective leader allows exceptions to the rule for exceptional results."[20]

Coach Wooden's advice is to be tolerant of the unconventional ideas and approaches of others as long as they don't negatively impact the rest of the organization or team. Don't get hung up on just one way of doing the little things. Focus on excellence, not just activity. Focus on results, not just on rules and doing things the so-called right way.

Whether you are a leader or a follower, a coach or a player, a boss or an employee, your goal should always be the relentless pursuit of excellence. You can never quite achieve perfection, but you should never cease reaching for it. As Coach Wooden once reflected, "UCLA had four so-called perfect seasons (30–0) during my years as head coach, and yet we never played a perfect game. However, we never ceased striving for the perfect play, the perfect pass, the perfect game. And it all started, in my view, with teaching those under my leadership how to put on their sweat socks 'perfectly.'"[21]

The pursuit of excellence begins with careful attention to the little things.

7

Little Things
Guard Your Character

While I can't prove that a person of good character has more
potential as a team player . . . that's the person I want to coach.

Coach John Wooden

As a basketball player, Brad Holland just
missed the John Wooden era, playing at UCLA from
1976 through 1979. After a playing career with the Los
Angeles Lakers, he worked as a broadcaster and as head basketball coach at the University of San Diego. Brad told me about
an incident that impressed him deeply—an incident in which
he saw the sterling character of Coach John Wooden.

"We invited Coach Wooden to be the featured speaker at a
fund-raising dinner," Brad told me. "We had earmarked fifteen
thousand dollars for Coach Wooden's speaking fee. I called
Coach and made the offer to him. He said, 'Brad, I'll come on
one condition. You take that fifteen thousand dollars and tell

them to put it back into your athletic program.' That's the way Coach was. He was always generous, always giving back. In a world full of takers, Coach John Wooden proved that nice guys sometimes finish first."

Dick Ridgeway played basketball for Coach Wooden in the 1950s. When he died at age thirty-nine, he left a wife and two young boys behind. His widow, Diane Ridgeway Cloud, told me how devastated and alone she felt immediately after losing her husband. "We had a small private service in Claremont, California. I don't know who told John Wooden about Dick's death, but he seemed to swoop in out of nowhere. He took my two sons by the hand and led them on a thirty-minute walk around the cemetery. I could see him talking to the boys as they walked, but to this day I have no idea what he told them. I just know they have never forgotten Coach Wooden's kindness."

John Wooden exemplified good character, having learned the importance of good character during his formative years. One of the most important character lessons he learned as a boy had to do with one of the little things in life—a five-cent bottle of cream soda.

One summer during his elementary school years, young Johnny Wooden and his friend Freddy walked to Breedlove's General Store in Centerton, Indiana. It was a hot, humid summer day, and both boys were terribly thirsty. That was no problem for Freddy, because he had his parents' permission to charge a nickel bottle of soda pop to his family's account anytime he wished. Johnny, the son of struggling farming parents, knew he didn't have permission to charge anything, not even a nickel. He tried to resist temptation, but his throat was so parched and it was so hot outside, and Freddy's bottle of soda pop looked so cold and refreshing.

Finally, Johnny gave in, took a frosty bottle of cream soda out of the cooler, and told the man at the counter, "Charge it."

At first, that cold cream soda tasted sweeter than anything he had ever tasted before. But as the final gulp went down, the guilt set in, mingled with fear of the punishment he would receive when his father found out. Johnny's conscience troubled him until he finally went to his parents and confessed his five-cent crime.

Years later, John Wooden recalled, "Dad and Mother understood my being tempted, and they just explained firmly why my actions were wrong. Believe me, that made a big impression on me and I never did anything like that again."[1]

Character Is Made of Little Things

Your character is the sum total of your enduring moral attributes. Character consists of such traits as honesty, integrity, courage, work ethic, persistence, loyalty, faithfulness, and more. The development of these traits is the result of a process of personality formation—a process consisting of all the moral decisions we make, in matters both small and great, throughout our lives. At every moral decision point in our lives, we have a choice to become stronger in our character or weaker and less virtuous. Every morally sound decision contributes to a stronger and more dependable character.

The word *character* is derived from an ancient Greek word that refers to an image stamped onto a coin. Over time, the accumulation of all the moral decisions we make stamps a pattern or image onto our lives. A person who makes consistently honest choices develops a personality marked by the character trait of honesty. You can place that person under the most extreme temptation imaginable, assure him he will never get caught, and he will still make the honest choice. Why? Because he is a person of honest character. To lie or steal would be to violate the essence of who he is.

The apostle Paul in the New Testament views character as a spiritual issue and calls good character traits "the fruit of the Spirit"—that is, the results of living according to the leading of God's Spirit. Paul writes, "But the fruit of the Spirit is love, joy, peace, forbearance, kindness, goodness, faithfulness, gentleness and self-control. Against such things there is no law" (Gal. 5:22–23).

Clearly, many qualities and traits make up good character. As Coach Wooden once wrote, "You can be as honest as the day is long and still be short on character. How? You can be honest and selfish, honest and undisciplined, honest and inconsistent, honest and disrespectful, honest and lazy. . . . There's more to character than just being honest."[2]

Few of us realize the awesome power we possess through the ability to make moral choices. We rarely stop to think of where our choices might take us. The right moral choice could set us on a pathway to success and fulfillment. The wrong moral choice could lead us to destruction. Even seemingly small moral choices often have vast consequences. We must not ignore the little things, because the little things have enormous power to set the course of our lives, just as a tiny rudder has the power to set the course of a mighty ocean liner.

If you maintain your moral character in the little things, you will never have your life and reputation destroyed by the big things. If you refuse to commit even a little white lie, then you will never go to prison for perjury. If you are never caught taking a pen or a paper clip from your employer's office, then you will never go to prison for embezzlement. By guarding your character in the little things, you make sure you can be trusted with the big things. As Jesus himself once said, "Whoever can be trusted with very little can also be trusted with much, and whoever is dishonest with very little will also be dishonest with much" (Luke 16:10).

Rick Warren, author of *The Purpose Driven Life*, put it this way:

> We think it's the big things in life that create a leader—no. The big crises in life reveal leadership, but leadership is not built in the big things of life. It's built in the small things of life. That's where integrity shows up—in the stuff that nobody sees, in the stuff behind the scenes. In the small, unseen, unspectacular choices of life where you do the right thing even though nobody's ever going to see it.[3]

Most of us think we are pretty good people, and we don't engage in little sins. We consider ourselves to be highly ethical people, people of character. But if we honestly, searchingly examined all the little corners and crevices of our lives, what would we find? We might find we drive a little faster than we should and speed through yellow lights when we really ought to stop. We might find that we enjoy gossiping about other people a little more than we like to admit. We might find that we fudge our tax returns.

We would never commit adultery, but what about that "little" matter of internet pornography? We would never assault anyone, but what about that "little" matter of flipping an obscene gesture to that "idiot" on the freeway? We would never steal money from the boss's safe, but what about that "little" matter of the padded expense account?

As the late, great motivational author and speaker Zig Ziglar once put it, "Earthquakes and hurricanes get all the publicity, but termites do more damage than both of them combined and the termite takes bites so small that you cannot see them with the naked eye. However, termites are persistent, they take lots of bites, and there are lots of termites." What are the "termites" Ziglar referred to? Little sins and character flaws.[4]

The Safest Road to Hell

In *The Screwtape Letters*, C. S. Lewis describes a senior demon named Screwtape advising his nephew, the minor demon Wormwood, on how to make sure a man remains bound by sin and separated from God (Screwtape calls God "the Enemy"). The demon writes:

> You will say that these are very small sins; and doubtless, like all young tempters, you are anxious to be able to report spectacular wickedness. But do remember, the only thing that matters is the extent to which you separate the man from the Enemy. It does not matter how small the sins are provided that their cumulative effect is to edge the man away from the Light and out into the Nothing. Murder is no better than cards if cards can do the trick. Indeed the safest road to Hell is the gradual one—the gentle slope, soft underfoot, without sudden turnings, without milestones, without signposts.[5]

Lewis understood the power of those subtle, little acts of corruption that threaten our character. Every little sin is truly a skirmish, a scuffle, a single clash in a never-ending struggle for control of this battlefield called our souls. Every day, we are bombarded by choices. Every hour, we are required to make a choice between good or evil. It may only be a minor good or a seemingly inconsequential evil, but our character is made up of these seemingly little choices. Our eternal destiny is decided, moment by moment, by the little decisions we make on a daily and hourly basis. In *Mere Christianity*, C. S. Lewis put it this way:

> Good and evil both increase at compound interest. That is why the little decisions you and I make every day are of such infinite importance. The smallest good act today is the capture of a strategic point from which, a few months later, you may be able to go on to victories you never dreamed of. An apparently trivial indulgence in lust or anger today is the loss of a ridge or

railway line or bridgehead from which the enemy may launch an attack otherwise impossible.[6]

Lewis offered an example from World War II and the terrible cruelty of Nazi Germany to show how small evils can grow at compound interest into monstrous evils, how feelings of hatred can fan the flames of a Holocaust: "The Germans, perhaps, at first ill-treated the Jews because they hated them: afterwards they hated them much more because they had ill-treated them. The more cruel you are, the more you will hate; and the more you hate, the more cruel you will become—and so on in a vicious circle for ever."[7]

Pastor Dave Egner recalls a time when he and his son bought an old powerboat to use for weekend fishing. When they tried the boat out on the water, it wouldn't run properly. They couldn't get the boat to accelerate to full speed, and it would shudder and vibrate at even modest speeds. They tried cleaning out the fuel system, adjusting the carburetor, and changing the fuel filter, but nothing worked.

Finally, Egner's son noticed a small nick in one of the propeller blades and suggested that the nick might be to blame. The nick was only three-fourths of an inch long. Egner was sure that such a tiny flaw in the propeller blade couldn't possibly be the problem, but they had tried everything else. He installed a new propeller, and they tried the boat on the water. The boat ran as smooth as silk, accelerating easily up to full speed, no shudders, no vibrations. One tiny nick in a propeller blade had rendered the entire boat useless. To make the boat useful again, that tiny flaw had to be eliminated.

Seemingly "little" sins and "tiny" character flaws can have the same effect on our lives. If we tolerate these little defects in our character, they will corrupt our thinking and our behavior, making us dysfunctional and unusable. Little nicks in our character can cause big trouble.[8]

Coach Wooden understood the need to terminate little sins before they grow into big character flaws. He first learned this lesson over a nickel bottle of soda pop. He passed this lesson along to his players by every means possible, including such maxims as, "Be more concerned with your character than your reputation, because your character is what you really are, while your reputation is merely what others think you are." And, "Ability may get you to the top, but it takes character to keep you there." And, "Tell the truth. That way you don't have to remember a story."[9]

The character qualities Coach Wooden's players learned from him gave them an edge on the basketball court. Even more importantly, those character qualities gave them an edge in the game of life.

Fifty Thousand Individual Decisions

Dennis De Haan tells a story about a woman who lived many years ago in Hanover, Germany. She claimed not to believe in the Christian doctrine of the resurrection, yet she also feared that the resurrection might actually take place—and she wanted no part of it. In her will, she directed that she be buried in a grave beneath two huge slabs of granite fastened together with massive steel clamps. She also ordered that the headstone be engraved with these words: "This burial place must never be opened."

If you go to the Hanover cemetery, you can find this woman's grave today. You will see that the heavy granite slabs have been displaced from their original position, and the massive steel clamps have been pulled out of their sockets. The woman believed that she had found a way to cheat the resurrection with immovable stone and unyielding steel, but the stone has already moved and the steel has already yielded.

What shifted them? An earthquake? A stray blockbuster bomb dropped during World War II? Powerful earth-moving equipment? No, the stone and the steel were not moved by big things. They were moved by little things. A tiny seed germinated at the edge of one of the stone slabs. No one took notice as the seed grew into a seedling, then into a small tree that sent out tiny roots. As the tree grew, as the roots spread, the granite slabs slowly shifted, the steel clamps were forced upward. The massive stones and steel bands yielded to the life force of a little thing.[10]

In our lives, we tend to focus on the big things. We focus on our career goals, our finances, our daily schedules, world events, and so forth. We would do well, from time to time, to pause and pay attention to the little things that can, over time, exert a massive influence over the course of our lives. If we make good decisions in all the little things of our lives, the accumulation of all those little choices will produce a huge and positive effect in our character and in the course of our lives. But if we are inattentive, if we make a lot of little decisions toward selfishness, greed, dishonesty, immorality, and expediency, we will one day look back and see that all those "insignificant" choices have taken a terrible toll on our lives, our relationships, and our souls.

Jaroldeen Edwards, author of *Celebration!*, describes what she has called the daffodil principle. The term comes from a unique five-acre spot high in the San Bernardino Mountains of Southern California known as the Daffodil Garden. The garden—all five acres of it—was planted by one woman named Gene Bauer. She began planting daffodil bulbs in 1958.

Edwards describes how her daughter Carolyn had repeatedly urged her to take the two-hour drive from Laguna, in Orange County, California, to Lake Arrowhead to see the daffodils. But Edwards really didn't want to drive two hours just to see a field of flowers. Finally, she gave in to Carolyn's pleas and drove to the mountains. When she got there, the weather was cold and rainy, and she knew she wouldn't be able to see the flowers. So she decided to simply spend her time visiting with her daughter and her grandchildren.

But Carolyn insisted. "Mother," she said, "you will never forgive yourself if you miss this experience."

So Edwards gave in and let her daughter drive her up the road in the rain. After twenty minutes, they reached a gravel road where there was a small church and a hand-lettered sign that read, "Daffodil Garden." They stopped and got out of the car. During a break in the rain, Edwards, Carolyn, and Carolyn's children started down the path together. They turned a corner, and Edwards gasped.

"Before me lay the most glorious sight," she later recalled. "It looked as though someone had taken a great vat of gold and poured it over the mountain peak and its surrounding slopes. There were five acres of flowers."

She turned to her daughter and asked, "Who did this?"

"Just one woman," Carolyn said. "That's her home." She pointed to an A-frame cabin in the midst of the Daffodil Garden. They walked together toward the modest little house, and Edwards saw a sign posted on the porch. It read:

Answers to the Questions
I Know You Are Asking:

50,000 Bulbs

One at a Time, by One Woman.

Two Hands, Two Feet, and One Brain.

Began in 1958.

One woman, starting decades earlier, planting one bulb at a time, had transformed a mountaintop. By the power of a lot of little things done well, by making fifty thousand individual decisions—"I will plant this daffodil bulb in this spot right now"—she had created a vision of indescribable beauty and magnificence. One woman, Gene Bauer, had created that five-acre garden the same way you and I must build and guard our character—through a series of small decisions made one after another over a long period of time. If we will do that, if we will remain attentive and focused on the little things, we will build a strong, durable character that will endure even through times of trial, stress, and temptation.

In late August and early September 1999—not very long after Jaroldeen Edwards first saw the Daffodil Garden—the Lake Arrowhead area of the San Bernardino Mountains was hit by a devastating weeklong wildfire known as the Willow Fire. It burned across the area of the Daffodil Garden, destroying Gene Bauer's A-frame house and the surrounding trees. The land that had once been brilliant with golden daffodils was blackened and scorched.

But the following spring, the green daffodil shoots sprang up from the ground, and within weeks the entire five acres was once again blindingly bright with golden daffodil blooms. The fire had destroyed everything else, but the fire could not destroy the daffodil bulbs in the ground, and the Daffodil Garden continues to blaze forth every spring to this day.[11]

What kind of character do you want to build? You may think, "At this point in my life, I've made so many bad choices that it's too late for me." No, it's not too late to start making good choices, moral choices, and start building and guarding your character. You simply need to become aware of the power of little choices, and you have to start making good decisions in all the little things of your life. Make that commitment today, renew that commitment every day, and you will begin to transform your life into a garden of character traits that will endure even through the wildfires of this life.

Wisdom from Two Sets of Threes

In an earlier book, *Coach Wooden: The Seven Principles That Shaped His Life and Will Change Yours*, I described how the sterling character of Coach John Wooden can largely be traced to a piece of paper his father, Joshua Hugh Wooden, gave him on the day Johnny graduated from the eighth grade. Coach Wooden's father was not a rich man, so the only gifts he could give his son were (as Coach later recalled) "a two-dollar bill, and a small card with a poem on one side and seven rules for living on the other." Those seven rules were instructions in maintaining one's character by being attentive to the little things in life:

1. Be true to yourself.
2. Help others.
3. Make each day your masterpiece.
4. Drink deeply from good books, especially the Bible.
5. Make friendship a fine art.
6. Build a shelter against a rainy day by the life you live.
7. Pray for guidance and counsel, and give thanks for your blessings each day.

The day Joshua Hugh Wooden gave that piece of paper to twelve-year-old Johnny, he said, "Son, try to live up to this." Johnny Wooden tucked that paper in his wallet and kept it with him throughout his life. (He also kept that two-dollar bill and later handed it down to his own son, Jim Wooden.)[12]

Joshua Hugh Wooden also taught Johnny and his three brothers what he called the Two Sets of Threes. The first set: Never lie. Never cheat. Never steal. The second set: Don't whine. Don't complain. Don't make excuses. Over the years, Coach John Wooden taught those seven rules and the Two Sets of Threes to all his players.[13]

Coach Wooden is probably best known for his Pyramid of Success, a concept he first began developing in the 1930s. The Pyramid is a visual representation of the character qualities needed to become successful in any endeavor in life. Coach Wooden once called it "the only truly original thing I have ever done."[14] It is made up of five rows of building blocks of character, starting at the base or foundation level and working up to the pinnacle.

The foundation row of building blocks consists of industriousness, friendship, loyalty, cooperation, and enthusiasm. The second level consists of self-control, alertness, initiative, and intentness. The third level consists of condition, skill, and team spirit. The fourth level consists of poise and confidence. The pinnacle is competitive greatness. Coach Wooden defined competitive greatness as performing at your peak ability when your very best is required. He would quickly add that your best is required of you every single day.

Coach Wooden summed up the message of his Pyramid of Success by defining what success truly means. "Success," he said, "is peace of mind, which is a direct result of self-satisfaction in knowing you made the effort to become the best of which you are capable."[15]

In order to be successful, we must make a consistent, daily effort to do our best in everything we do, including all the little things. Here are some principles to guide you in your decision making in the small things so that you can become a person of great character and integrity:

- *There are no insignificant moral choices; your "little" decisions invariably impact your life in a big way.* Young Johnny Wooden made a poor decision in purchasing a nickel bottle of cream soda, but he followed that poor decision with a good decision to tell his parents what he had done. He never forgot those two decisions about a seemingly insignificant matter, and that incident helped to shape his moral character throughout the rest of his life.

- *Character is much more than merely being honest.* To be a person of character, focus daily on such character traits as self-discipline, hard work, courage, perseverance, faithfulness, gentleness, and kindness.

- *Most of us give ourselves more credit for character than we deserve.* Take a fearless moral inventory of your life and ask yourself, Am I truly as honest as I think I am, or do I lie and deceive others in the little things of my life? Am I truly as kind and thoughtful as I think I am, or do I engage in gossip and harming other people's reputations? Am I truly as moral and upright as I think I am, or am I unfaithful to God and to my spouse in my thoughts? Until we can honestly say we have sterling character in the little things of life, we can't truly claim to be people of character at all.

- *You should never mistake your reputation for your character.* Coach Wooden said, "Be more concerned with your character than your reputation, because your character is what you really are, while your reputation is merely what others think you are."[16] You need to always make sure that you are at least as concerned about the inner reality of your character as the outer image of your reputation. If your reputation exceeds your character, you are a hypocrite. You need to make sure that your reputation is an accurate representation of who you really are as a person of character.

- *Character is formed through the hundreds, if not thousands, of tiny decisions you make throughout each day.* Just as a woman created five acres of daffodils by planting fifty thousand bulbs one at a time, you create your character by the many decisions you make in your life every single day. Each decision you make helps to cement the kind of person you will be for the rest of your life. Every time you make a decision, no matter how small, think about the consequences for your character.

- *Always remember the Two Sets of Threes formulated by Coach John Wooden's father.* The first set: Never lie. Never cheat. Never steal. The second set: Don't whine. Don't complain. Don't make excuses. If you live by the Two Sets of Threes, you will always make quality decisions, and you can't help but become a person of excellent character.

Coach Wooden demonstrated his unyielding integrity in 1948, when he was a teacher and coach at Indiana State Teachers' College. He received offers to serve as the head basketball coach at two schools, the University of Minnesota and UCLA. He loved the Midwest and wanted to accept the position at Minnesota, but there were some matters to be resolved by the Minnesota board of directors before he could say yes. Meanwhile, UCLA was pressing him for an answer. So Coach arranged for the University of Minnesota to phone him at 6 p.m. on a Saturday night and for UCLA to phone him an hour later. This way, he would know if he had a firm offer from the University of Minnesota before he gave his answer to UCLA.

Saturday night came. Coach awaited the call from Minnesota, but the phone didn't ring. Promptly at 7 p.m., UCLA called and offered him the job. Coach Wooden concluded that the University of Minnesota was no longer interested, so he accepted the post at UCLA. Moments after accepting UCLA's offer, the phone rang again. It was the University of Minnesota. A massive ice storm had knocked out the phone lines all across Minnesota, and the board members from Minnesota had been trying for ninety minutes to get through. Minnesota had enthusiastically agreed to Coach Wooden's conditions. The job was his if he wanted it.

Coach Wooden wanted that job very much, but he said no. He was taking the position at UCLA.

Many would say that Coach Wooden should have simply called UCLA back and said he had changed his mind. After all, he had only agreed verbally and hadn't signed a contract. If UCLA didn't have it in writing, they couldn't hold him to it. But Coach Wooden didn't even consider such a possibility. He had given his word. The notion of breaking his word was no more thinkable to him than the notion that he could fly by flapping his arms. It simply could not be done.

More importantly, Coach Wooden is convinced that by keeping his word and guarding his character, he allowed God to take his life in a direction he might not have chosen for himself. A Minnesota ice storm, combined with John Wooden's unbending integrity, sent him to sunny California, where Coach Wooden earned an unmatched record of ten NCAA championships and a reputation as the greatest coach of all time.

As Coach himself later reflected, "If fate had not intervened, I would never have gone to UCLA. But my dad's little set of threes served me well: 'Don't whine. Don't complain. Don't make excuses.' . . . Things turn out best for those who make the best of the way things turn out."[17]

As former UCLA student manager George Morgan once told me, "The John Wooden at practice was the same John Wooden in the locker room. The John Wooden in the locker room was the same John Wooden on the campus. The John Wooden on the campus was the same John Wooden at home." Coach Wooden exemplified good character in all the little things, and that was the secret of his greatness in the big things.

8

Little Things Yield
a Habit of Success

The four laws of learning are explanation, demonstration, imitation, and repetition. The goal is to create a correct habit that can be produced instinctively under great pressure. To make sure this goal is achieved, I created eight laws of learning; namely, explanation, demonstration, imitation, repetition, repetition, repetition, repetition, and repetition.

Coach John Wooden

SWEN NATER SHARED A STORY WITH ME FROM HIS UCLA playing days. He and his teammates were on the floor of Pauley Pavilion about to begin basketball practice with Coach Wooden. While warming up, Nater saw one of his teammates walk into the arena in his street clothes and talk privately with Coach Wooden.

That was baffling. Why didn't the guy dress for practice? And what were he and Coach Wooden discussing in quiet tones? It was almost unheard of for a player to be late for practice. Coach Wooden made practice *fun*. So when a player showed up late for practice, something was definitely wrong.

Turning to teammate Kenny Booker, Nater asked, "What's up? Why is that guy late?"

"You didn't hear?" Booker said. "He has fifteen unpaid parking tickets from campus police, and they finally caught up with him." Booker nodded toward the rest of the team. "We all knew he'd be late today."

Nater was floored. "Did Coach know?" he asked.

"Are you kidding?" Booker said. "Coach knows *everything* before we do."

Coach Wooden's policy on tardiness had the force of law among the Bruins players: If a player knew he'd be late for practice, he needn't bother dressing for practice. Instead, he had to show up in street clothes to present his excuse. If Coach accepted the excuse, the player could then dress for practice. If not, Coach could, at his sole discretion, dismiss the player for the day. "Practice," Coach often said, "is a privilege."

If you've ever played sports at any level, you probably had a coach who disciplined tardiness and other infractions with a physical punishment, such as running laps or doing push-ups. Or you might have had a coach who would make you sweep the gym or pick up trash. Coach Wooden never used the threat of punishment. He would simply withhold the privilege of practice. And that was enough.

Coach Wooden didn't want his players to fear him as a disciplinarian. He did not want to impose external discipline on the team. Rather, he wanted his players to be motivated and disciplined from within. He used his players' natural desire to compete as an incentive for them to build good habits and self-discipline. As Coach often said, "Discipline yourself and others won't need to."

Winning Is a Habit

"If you are going to achieve excellence in big things," General Colin Powell once observed, "you develop the habit in little matters. Excellence is not an exception, it is a prevailing attitude."[1] These are wise words that echo the success principles of Coach John Wooden. Mediocre people consider excellence to be an exceptional achievement, but successful people consider excellence to be a continuous, habitual, moment-by-moment commitment to doing a lot of little things well.

Motivational speaker Joel Weldon reminds us that it is the little habits, the little unhealthy impulses, the seemingly minor patterns and proclivities, the troublesome quirks and self-defeating attitudes that can keep us from achieving our goals. We can usually overcome the big stuff; it's the small stuff that so often trips us up. In a speech called "Elephants Don't Bite!," Weldon said, "Raise your hand if you have ever been bitten by a mosquito. . . . Has anyone here been bitten by an elephant? . . . That proves my point! It's the little things that get you, not the big things. The little things come along and cause big problems. And it's the little things you do right that can bring you huge rewards."[2]

We are creatures of habit, and our habits tend to define who we are, for better or for worse. We come into the world without a single habit. We accumulate habits over time. We perform an action once, then again, then again, and then that action becomes a habit. Some of our habits are good and healthy and lead us toward a successful life. Other habits are harmful and unhealthy and tend to hold us back from living effectively. The nineteenth-century preacher Tryon Edwards, author of *A Dictionary of Thoughts*, observed, "Any act often repeated soon forms a habit; and habit allowed, steady gains in strength. At first it may be but as the spider's web, easily broken through, but if not resisted it soon binds us with chains of steel."[3] Another nineteenth-century preacher, Nathaniel Emmons, put it this way: "Habit is either the best of servants, or the worst of masters."[4]

Even though we are fully, painfully aware of some of our worst habits, we find it difficult to break them. Many of us feel defeated by our habits and helpless to overcome them. Yet it is truly our habits, the little things we do again and again, day by day, that determine whether we will be successful in life. As motivational writer Og Mandino wrote in *The Greatest Secret in the World*, "In truth, the only difference between those who have failed and those who have succeeded lies in the difference of their habits. Good habits are the key to all success. Bad habits are the unlocked door to failure. Thus, the first law I will obey, which precedeth all others is—*I will form good habits and become their slave.*"[5]

Examine the lives of successful people, and you will see this principle played out again and again: successful people make a continuous habit of doing a lot of little things well, again and again and again. Industrialist and philanthropist J. Paul Getty, founder of the Getty Oil Company, once expressed the principle that defined his life: "The individual who wants to reach the top in business must appreciate the might and force of habit. He must be quick to break those habits that can break him—and hasten to adopt those practices that will become the habits that help him achieve the success he desires."[6]

John Jacob Astor (1763–1848), the German immigrant business magnate who became America's first multimillionaire, explained his success this way:

> The man who makes it the habit of his life to go to bed at nine o'clock, usually gets rich and is always reliable. Of course, going to bed does not make him rich—I merely mean that such a man will in all probability be up early in the morning and do a big day's work, so his weary bones put him to bed early. Rogues do

their work at night. Honest men work by day. It's all a matter of habit, and good habits in America make any man rich. Wealth is a result of habit.[7]

Motivational author Brian Tracy tells of a businessman, Herbert Grey, who went on an eleven-year quest for the "common denominator of success." At the end of his research, Grey concluded that there was one unmistakable difference between successful people and unsuccessful people. "Successful people," Tracy said, "make a habit of doing what unsuccessful people don't like to do."

Tracy was quick to add that successful people don't like doing those things either, but they have disciplined themselves to habitually do the things that lead to success, whether they like doing them or not. Successful people may not like rising early, working hard, staying late, taking risks, enduring rejection, and stepping out of their comfort zone, but they willingly and habitually do the hard tasks, the unpleasant tasks, knowing that this is the price they must pay to rise above mediocrity and achieve success.[8]

Herbert Grey and Brian Tracy described a principle that the late Green Bay Packers coach Vince Lombardi famously set forth in a speech to his players: "Winning," he said, "is not a sometime thing; it's an all-the-time thing. You don't win once in a while, you don't do things right once in a while, you do them right all the time. Winning is a habit. Unfortunately, so is losing."[9] Therefore, our goal in life must be to build winning habits into our lives.

How to Break a Bad Habit

Author and screenwriter Gene Fowler was a friend to many Hollywood celebrities, including John Barrymore, W. C. Fields, and Red Skelton. Fowler's biographer, Harry Allen Smith, tells of the time in 1951 when Fowler and his wife, Agnes, flew to Europe with Red Skelton and a number of Hollywood friends. Skelton was scheduled to perform his comedy act at the London Palladium, but he wanted to take the Fowlers and other friends on a European tour before going on to London. After several days in Rome, Skelton, the Fowlers, and their friends boarded a four-engine airliner for the flight north.

As the plane took them over the Swiss Alps, one of the engines failed. Minutes later, a second engine failed. Then a third engine failed, leaving the plane with only one engine and nothing below them but rugged alpine mountains. The situation seemed dire, and the passengers—who had never been devout believers before—began to pray for deliverance. To encourage his fellow passengers and distract them from their predicament, Skelton stood in the aisle and performed his comedy routine.

As the remaining engine began to sputter, the pilot spotted a broad field of clover directly ahead, surrounded by steep mountain crags. The pilot brought the crippled plane in for a perfect, feather-light landing. After the plane rolled to a stop, all the passengers were silent, contemplating their close brush with death.

Skelton broke the silence, saying, "Now, ladies and gentlemen, you may all return to the evil habits you gave up just twenty minutes ago."[10]

Bad habits are easy to give up when we are flying over the Alps on one engine and a prayer. It's much harder to give up bad habits during the normal course of our everyday lives. As motivational writer Hal Urban explains:

Trying to break a bad habit through sheer willpower rarely works. What has proven to be far more effective is replacing the habit—substituting it with a behavior that is more positive. This technique has been around for hundreds of years, at least as far back as Benjamin Franklin's time. In his famous autobiography, Franklin explains a technique he used for eliminating his worst habits and replacing them with good ones. He made a list of thirteen qualities he wanted to have. He put them in order of importance and wrote each one on a separate page in a small notebook. He concentrated on each quality for a week at a time. . . . By using this technique, Franklin's new habits replaced some of his old ones. He eliminated a set of behaviors that worked against him while acquiring another set that was more beneficial to him. He said it made him realize that he had more faults than he'd originally thought, but the experience had also given him great satisfaction in seeing their replacements take over.[11]

Fred Smith Sr. was a business consultant, speaker, and mentor to many executives and leaders, including Billy Graham, John Maxwell, Ken Blanchard, Zig Ziglar, Charlie "Tremendous" Jones, and me. I once heard Fred tell a story that illustrates the effect of bad habits in our lives. He recalled boarding a Boeing 707 airliner for a flight from Los Angeles to Miami. As the plane sat on the tarmac, preparing for takeoff, Fred anticipated the roar of the engines and the feeling of acceleration. He always enjoyed that sensation of power as a plane took off.

But on this particular occasion, when he heard the engines roar to life, he looked out the window and saw that the scenery was passing by in the wrong direction. The big jet was moving backward! Looking out the window toward the rear of the plane, Fred saw that a tractor was hooked up to the tail of the aircraft and was pulling the jet backward, even as the engines were revving up.

It occurred to Fred that he was witnessing a metaphor of his own life. "Fred," he told himself, "this jetliner is just like you. You get your engines running, you've got plenty of power to go forward, but you are letting some old habit, some foolish flaw in your character, get hold of you and pull you backward, away from your goals. Fred, you've got to identify those bad habits, those 'tractors' in your life that are holding you back, and you've got to cut the tether and start soaring the way you were meant to."

It's true. Our bad habits hold us back from our goals and prevent us from achieving all we were meant to achieve. Our bad habits keep us mired in mediocrity.

Retired NBA player and former NBA head coach Avery Johnson witnessed the constructive power of good habits and the destructive power of bad habits from both sides of the coach's whistle. He observes that it is important for us all to reflect on our lives and to take stock of both our good habits and our bad habits:

> We must take a self-inventory and determine what we must do to win. I learned at the tender age of forty-two that we all have two habits we need to *stop* doing, two habits we need to *keep* doing, and two habits we need to *start* doing. Ask yourself where you are and, if you are not satisfied with the answer, take an honest look at your habits. Chances are that there are habits that got you there and, most importantly, habits that will keep you where you are. There may be some habits you must eliminate if you are going to win.[12]

That's excellent advice. What habits do you need to stop doing? What habits do you need to keep doing? And what habits do you need to start doing? Let me suggest some ways to build good habits into your life.

Start Building Healthy Habits

As we learned from Hal Urban and his example of Benjamin Franklin's list of thirteen habits he sought to acquire, the best way to break a bad habit is to replace it with a good habit.

When we simply try to break a bad habit through the force of willpower alone, we find ourselves continually thinking about that habit—and then are tempted by it. But if we decide to replace a bad habit with a good habit, our thoughts are continually focused on that good habit. And that's a healthy focus to have. Here are some principles to keep in mind as you replace unhealthy habits with good habits:

- *Focus on little things.* Instead of trying to make big, sweeping changes in your life, focus on something small, simple, and manageable. For example, instead of saying, "I'm going to devote three hours a day to prayer," say, "I'm going to get up fifteen minutes earlier each morning and have a quiet time with God." Instead of saying, "I'm going to take the next three months to write the great American novel," say, "I'm going to spend fifteen minutes every night before I go to bed writing one page of my novel. With that as my habit, I'll have my novel finished in a year." Instead of saying, "I'm going to learn a language in a month," say, "I'm going to spend fifteen minutes each day with my language-learning program and become fluent in a year."

- *When you set too challenging a goal, you set yourself up for failure.* If you commit yourself to small changes, you set yourself up for a successful, healthy habit—a habit you'll be more likely to maintain for life.

- *Practice that habit faithfully and repeatedly.* Schedule it for the same time every day. Some experts claim that by repeating an action daily for twenty-one days or thirty days, you can turn that action into a habit. It may take you more time to develop a healthy habit, but the more faithfully you repeat an action, the easier it becomes for that action to become a habit—and the harder it becomes to break that healthy habit.

- *Post a reminder of your commitment to your new, healthy habit.* Make a little sign on an index card or a Post-it note, and put that sign where you will see it every day—say, on your bathroom mirror, the refrigerator door, or the dashboard of your car. A mental reminder is not enough. It helps to have a visual reminder that nags at you every time you see it.

- *Focus on one habit at a time.* Again, the key principle is to focus on the little things, the simple things, the doable things. If you take on too big a challenge, if you try to do too many things at once, you practically guarantee failure. You can build many new habits by building one habit at a time. Focus on one habit in January, a new one in February, another in March, and so forth. It's easy to keep adding one new habit at a time, but it's almost impossible to focus on many new habits at once. Be careful not to overwhelm yourself with too big a challenge.

- *Focus on adding good habits, not breaking bad habits.* Keep a positive focus on building good routines. As you add good habits to your life, they will replace the bad habits, and you will see those unhealthy habits simply fade from your life.

- *Go easy on yourself.* When you fall off the wagon and neglect a new habit or slip back into an old unhealthy habit, forgive yourself and start over. Ask God to forgive you and to give you the strength to keep going. Then pick up right where you left off and keep building that good habit into your life. Everybody has setbacks. Successful people don't let setbacks stop them.

- *Be flexible.* Building healthy new habits may be harder than you expect. You may find you need to adjust your expectations, try a different approach, schedule the activity differently, or ask someone for help in building the new habit. If you are flexible, you'll figure out what works for you, what doesn't work, and how to keep moving toward your goals. As you begin to build new habits, you'll be amazed at the positive change those habits produce. As the poet John Dryden once said, "We first make our habits, and then our habits make us."[13]

Now, let me suggest a number of positive, healthy habits that you may want to build into your life as part of your never-ending quest to become a person of excellence and achievement. These are the healthy habits that make the difference between a person of mediocrity and a person of excellence:

- *Awaken early*. Early risers get a jump on the rest of the world. The best way to control your day is to seize the day and seize it early.

- *Start each day with positive thoughts*. The morning is the perfect time to prepare yourself mentally for the day ahead, so start each day with a habit of positive, healthy thinking. The moment your eyes pop open, before you even roll out of bed, take time to thank God for the new day. The psalmist put it this way:

  > But I will sing of your strength,
  >   in the morning I will sing of your love;
  > for you are my fortress,
  >   my refuge in times of trouble.
  >
  > You are my strength, I sing praise to you;
  >   you, God, are my fortress,
  >   my God on whom I can rely. (Ps. 59:16–17)

- *Build a habit of daily exercise*. Exercise strengthens the body and sharpens the mind. Make a decision to exercise every day without fail. Your daily exercise session doesn't have to be strenuous or lengthy or painful. You don't need a gym membership or a weight machine in order to exercise. Walking is good exercise if you do it briskly and regularly. I don't recommend trying to make a habit of exercising three or four days a week. It's too easy to tell yourself, "I'll exercise tomorrow." If you know you have to exercise

153

every day, seven days a week, you'll find it harder to make excuses and easier to make a habit.

- *Build a habit of thankfulness.* Make gratitude a daily habit. Be grateful for the things that make life enjoyable. Thank God for your health, your freedom, your family and friends, and the opportunities you have to serve God and others. The more things you think of to be thankful for, the more grateful you will be.

- *Build a habit of learning something new every day.* Commit yourself to reading good books every day. Read about subjects you don't normally focus on. If you tend to read only trade magazines or popular culture magazines, go to the library and get some books on science, history, psychology, theology, or some other subject. Make a habit of widening your interests and broadening your knowledge.

- *Build a habit of smiling at people.* People who smile on the outside tend to be more optimistic and enthused on the inside. Smilers make a good impression on everyone around them. Smilers acknowledge others and create a positive vibe. In your home, around the office, at the store, or walking down the street, greet people with a warm, friendly smile. Make smiling your habit. You'll be amazed at how a little thing like a smile can change your life in big ways.

- *Build a habit of giving people sincere, heartfelt compliments.* Avoid empty praise that sounds phony. Never hesitate to say something to make another person feel great. People love to be complimented, and they like people who are generous and sincere with their compliments.

- *Build a habit of saying, "I love you."* Again, don't say it unless you mean it. But if you mean it, if you feel it, say it boldly. Don't assume people know you care about them. Tell your spouse and your children, again and again, "I love you," and find new and unique ways to communicate your love. And don't hesitate to tell friends and extended family you love them too. Life is too short to take loved ones for granted. So make it a daily habit to tell people how you really feel.

- *Build a habit of truly listening to other people.* When you have a conversation with your wife, your husband, your children, your friends, your co-workers, your boss, or your employees, look them in the eye and really listen. Put away that smart phone. If you receive a call or a text message, don't interrupt your conversation. Check your phone later. As you listen to people, nod, smile, give verbal feedback, ask pertinent questions to draw them out, and let them know you really hear them. Resist the temptation to cut them off, finish their sentences, or minimize and dismiss what they are saying. Build a habit of being a good listener.

- *Build a habit of carefully considering requests for your time before you say yes.* One of the most unhealthy habits people get into is saying yes to every request that comes along. By saying yes to someone else's priorities, you may well be saying no to your own goals and success. Instead of immediately answering yes or no, you can say, "Let me think about that," or, "Let me check my schedule." If you determine that you really need to say no to a request, get back to that person as soon as possible, tell him or her no politely but firmly, and say it in as few words as possible. Don't feel obligated to make an excuse or give an explanation. You have a right to set your own priorities and maintain your own schedule without explaining yourself to others. Learning to say no is a very good habit.

- *Build a habit of saving money.* A good rule of thumb is to set aside at least 10 percent of every paycheck in long-term savings. If you are not able to save 10 percent of your paycheck, you need to figure out where that money is going. If you find out that too much of your pay is being spent on entertainment, restaurant meals, and lattes at Starbucks, then you have a bad habit of overspending. You need to replace that overspending habit with a healthy saving habit.

- *Build a habit of spending significant time with your family.* Turn off your smart phone. Take an hour or two away from texting and updating your social media. Get out the board games or the bicycles, or just sit back with your family and talk. At first, you'll probably feel anxious and uneasy as you experience withdrawal from your mobile communication devices. That's okay. It's a good habit to give up social media cold turkey for a while. After your family time, those text messages will still be there—and your family needs you more than anyone who happens to be texting you.

- *Build a habit of tidying up every day.* Clean up the clutter where you work and where you live on a daily basis. A cluttered environment produces cluttered thinking, and messy surroundings are depressing. A clean environment keeps you sharp and focused on your goals, and clear thinking leads to success. A daily habit of keeping your workspace and living space clean and orderly contributes to a positive, can-do mind-set. Teach your kids to keep their workspaces and living spaces clean as well. Set a good example, put healthy routines in place, teach kids to be responsible, and build healthy habits of order and cleanliness in yourself and your entire family.

- *Build a daily habit of writing out a to-do list.* We all accomplish more each day when we have a written set of goals and priorities for the day. Some people make out their to-do list first thing in the morning. I find it even more helpful to make out my list the night before. Then, as soon as I get up, I have my list in front of me, and I'm ready to leap into my day. Use your list to prioritize your tasks, then stick to your priorities and get things done in the proper order—first things first. Tackle each priority in turn, complete it, cross it off the list, and go on to the next priority. Use that list to control your day. If an "emergency" rears its ugly head, consider where that "emergency" fits into your to-do list. Don't let urgent (but less important) problems scramble your priorities.

- *Build a habit to review each day before you go to bed.* Ask yourself, "What did I accomplish today? What did I do well? What could I have done better? Did I move closer to my goals? Did I stick to my priorities? Did I complete my to-do list? If I departed from my priorities, did I do so for a good reason?" (After all, it's often important to be flexible and responsive when a truly important need interrupts your schedule.) You can easily combine a nightly review of the day's accomplishments with making out your to-do list for the next day. A habit of reviewing the day's accomplishments and planning the next day's priorities can be a powerful tool in helping you focus on your most important goals.

- *Build a habit of hitting the sack at a reasonable time.* Undisciplined people often fiddle around and waste time before going to bed. They lose valuable, irreplaceable sleep, and they pay for it the next day by oversleeping or by simply feeling miserable. Have a regular bedtime, then get up early, ready to take on the day. Most people with this habit are highly productive and successful people.

Finally, let me share with you Brian Tracy's "Two Habits for Rapid Advancement." In his book *Million Dollar Habits*, he offers two simple habits that anyone can build and that will serve you well at any level in an organization, whether in the mail room or the board room.

The first habit for rapid advancement is this: be an exceptional worker. A forty-hour workweek is for average people. If you are willing to settle for being average, then go ahead and put in your average forty hours per week. But if you are committed to being exceptional and successful, don't settle for average. Instead, build exceptional work habits into your life. Tracy explains:

> If the workday starts at 8:30 a.m., you should be at work and busy by 8 o'clock. You should work steadily all day long. If the

workday ends at 5 o'clock, you should continue working until 5:30 or 6:00, or even later. The simple act of starting earlier, working harder, and staying later will increase your productivity by anything from 50 to 100 percent. The people who are in the best position to help you get ahead will soon notice these work habits. They will give you an edge over any of your coworkers.[14]

This doesn't mean you should work so long and so late that you neglect your family. With careful management of your time, you can be an available spouse, an involved parent, *and* an exceptional worker.

Tracy's second habit for rapid advancement is this: go to your employer and say you want more responsibility. You're not asking for a raise or a promotion or a title or recognition. You're simply asking for more responsibility. Tracy says, "Say you very much like your job, and you want to make an even more valuable contribution to the company." You'll be amazed at how quickly you'll advance in the organization when you let it be known that you want more responsibility.[15]

These, then, are the habits you need to be successful in your family, to be successful as a parent, to be successful in business, and to be successful in life. These are the habits of highly successful people. How many of these habits do you excel in? How many do you need to strengthen? How many do you need to acquire?

The Biggest Test of Your Life

In May 1993, former president Ronald Reagan gave the commencement address to the graduating class at the Citadel, the military college of South Carolina. During that speech, he told the story of a hero named Arland Williams, who had graduated from the Citadel in 1957. The story of Williams's heroism was close to the heart of President Reagan because his act of bravery took place a short distance from the White House, almost exactly one year into Reagan's presidency.

On January 13, 1982, Air Florida Flight 90 took off in subfreezing weather from Washington National Airport. The plane's wings were inadequately deiced, and the aircraft failed to gain altitude. The plane struck the 14th Street Bridge over the Potomac, hitting six cars and killing four motorists on the bridge. Then the plane plunged into the icy Potomac and sank until nothing but the tail section remained visible. Only six people of the airliner's seventy-nine passengers and crew survived the initial crash. Those six managed to escape through a rear door of the plane, but on emerging, they found themselves facing almost certain death by drowning and hypothermia.

As Reagan told the story, Williams "survived the impact of the crash and found himself with a small group of other survivors struggling to stay afloat in the near-frozen river. And then, suddenly, there was hope—a park police helicopter appeared overhead, trailing a lifeline to the outstretched hands below, a lifeline that could carry but a few of the victims to the safety of the shore. News cameramen, watching helplessly, recorded the scene as the man in the water repeatedly handed the rope to the others, refusing to save himself."

Williams kept passing the rope to the other survivors and assisting in their rescue. He passed the rope to all five of his fellow surviving passengers, and the helicopter went back and forth from the wreck to the shore five times. On the sixth and final trip, the helicopter dropped the rescue rope for Williams himself, but he was no longer there. He had slipped beneath the surface of the Potomac.

Reagan said:

For months thereafter we knew him only as the "unknown hero." Then an exhaustive Coast Guard investigation conclusively established his identity. . . . Many of you here today know his name as well as I do, for his portrait now hangs with honor—as it indeed should—on this very campus; the campus where he once walked, as you have, through the Summerall Gate and along the Avenue of Remembrance. He was a young first classman with a crisp uniform and a confident stride on a bright spring morning, full of hopes and plans for the future. He never dreamed that his life's supreme challenge would come in its final moments, some twenty-five years later. . . . His name was Arland D. Williams Jr., the Citadel Class of 1957. He brought honor to his alma mater, and honor to his nation. . . . Greater love, as the Bible tells us, hath no man than to lay down his life for a friend.

Reagan went on to say that he told Williams's story in part to honor him but also to make a point about what each of us must do to prepare ourselves for the unexpected challenges of this life.

The most crucial of life's moments come like the scriptural "thief in the night." Suddenly and without notice, the crisis is upon us and the moment of choice is at hand—a moment fraught with import for ourselves, and for all who are depending on the choice we make. We find ourselves, if you will, plunged without warning into the icy water, where the currents of moral consequence run swift and deep, and where our fellow man—and yes, I believe, our Maker—are waiting to see whether we will pass the rope.

At such crucial moments, Reagan added, there is no time for debate, reflection, and a leisurely weighing of options. At such times, instinct, character, and habit take over. The core lesson of the life and death of Arland Williams is that

the character that takes command in moments of crucial choices has already been determined . . . by a thousand other choices made earlier in seemingly unimportant moments. It has been determined by all of the little choices of years past—by all those times when the voice of conscience was at war with the voice of temptation—whispering the lie that it really doesn't matter.

It has been determined by all of the day-to-day decisions made when life seemed easy and crises seemed far away—the decisions that, piece by piece, bit by bit, developed habits of discipline or of laziness, habits of self-sacrifice or of self-indulgence, habits of duty and honor and integrity—or dishonor and shame.

Because when life does get tough, and the crisis is undeniably at hand—when we must, in an instant, look inward for strength of character to see us through—we will find nothing inside ourselves that we have not already put there.[16]

What are we building in our lives every day by the thousands of decisions we make, by the habits we etch into our souls? What kind of future acts are we preparing ourselves for? Acts of heroism? Acts of honor and distinction? Or acts of selfishness, cowardice, and taking the easy way out? How will we respond when the crisis is upon us, we have no time to think, and habit takes over?

We are answering that question every single day, moment by moment, with every decision we make in the little things in life. The next time you face a decision about some seemingly insignificant moral choice, think about all the big things that hang in the balance. Think about the big decision you hope you'll make when you face the biggest test of your life.

We Are What We Repeatedly Do

Coach Wooden believed in teaching good habits by focusing on the little things. For example, he taught his players to respect themselves and respect others (which is a big thing) through such little things as picking up litter. He once explained his reasoning to a reporter:

> I like to make spot checks on lockers and see they're not getting slovenly. Wherever we are, we will leave our dressing rooms every

161

bit as neat as when we came in. There will be no gum wrappers on the floor. No tape scattered around. No orange peels. They'll all be placed in a container. And I don't expect our manager to be the pick-up man. Our players understand this.

I help. If I start picking things up, the players soon join in. We'll have equipment managers around the country tell us no one leaves the dressing room like we do. Well, I think that's part of better basketball. . . . I think it gives us a little more unity, a sense of doing things together, of showing consideration for the other fellow.[17]

Coach Wooden's larger goal was to create certain habits in his players—the habits that lead to winning. But the key to achieving that larger goal was careful attention to the little things. It meant being aware of gum wrappers and orange peels. And Coach Wooden himself led by personal example. When his players saw him stooping to pick up some trash on the locker room floor, they would not be outdone by their coach. They immediately joined in. Coach Wooden's example helped to build his players' awareness of the little things and to build a stronger esprit de corps.

As Coach Wooden once wrote, "I wanted to create good habits in those under my leadership, not only in the mechanics of playing basketball, but also in the fundamentals of being a good person. Thus, a small issue such as putting towels in the towel basket where they belonged was something I viewed as big, something that connected to my overall principles and beliefs."[18]

At the start of every season, Coach Wooden gave his players a piece of paper with the heading "Normal Expectations." How many expectations did Coach enumerate on that list? Just three—and they were little things, just three little rules of respect and common decency:

1. Be on time.
2. Do not use profanity at any time.
3. Never criticize a teammate.

Swen Nater, who played center for Coach Wooden from 1971 to 1973, is now an executive with Costco. He once told me, "I still live by the rules Coach taught me. Every time I leave a hotel room, I make sure the towels are picked up off the floor, the pillows are neatly placed on the bed, and every piece of trash is in the wastebaskets. Every morning when I get dressed, I put on my socks exactly as Coach taught us on our first day at UCLA. I put my toes in just so, adjust the heel, and smooth out the wrinkles. I do that whether I'm wearing basketball socks or business socks. And you know what? I've never had a blister, thanks to the little things Coach taught me when I was at UCLA."

By paying attention to such little things as these, Coach Wooden achieved great things: character growth, team unity, a commitment to building skills through consistent practice, and ultimately, an amazingly high winning percentage and championship banners hung from arena rafters.

We are the sum total of the habits we build over a lifetime of making decisions about the so-called little things in life. We are what we repeatedly do.

Don't wait until tomorrow to begin building the habits you need today. There is no time like the present to begin focusing on the little things that will enable you to build healthy habits. Don't delay. Start right now to make the decisions that build good habits. Be careful in all the little things of your life. Do that—and the big things will take care of themselves.

Epilogue

Life Is All about the Little Things

Develop a love of details. They usually accompany success.

Coach John Wooden

IN 1977, SEVEN-YEAR-OLD WILL MOSELLE ATTENDED Coach Wooden's summer basketball camp at Pepperdine University in Southern California. One morning before breakfast, young Moselle was on the basketball court, practicing free throws. "I could barely get the ball to the hoop," he recalled when I interviewed him.

Just then, Coach Wooden passed by, taking his early morning walk. "Coach came over," Moselle said, "and spent several minutes with me, working on my shooting form. I'm amazed to think back on it. The greatest coach in history took time to give private instruction to me, a little seven-year-old kid."

Moselle went on to attend UCLA, where he served as student manager for the Bruins under head coach Jim Harrick. One day,

Moselle was in the hall outside Coach Harrick's office when the long-retired Coach John Wooden happened to stop by.

"Coach engaged me in conversation about school, sports, and so forth for about ten minutes," Moselle recalled. "Just then, Coach Harrick came out of his office and said, 'Coach Wooden, come on in!' Coach Wooden said, 'Just a minute. Let me finish my conversation with Will.' By doing that, Coach conveyed to me that I was no less important than the head basketball coach at UCLA. That meant a lot to me."

It was a little gesture, but it made a big impression. Coach John Wooden never hesitated to acknowledge people and make them feel big. In his mind, there truly were no little people. Coach did not divide the human race into important people and unimportant people. Everybody was important to John Wooden.

Coach Wooden's nephew Kim Puckett told me another story that gives us a deep insight into Coach's appreciation of the little things, the simple pleasures of life. Once, while Puckett was visiting his uncle in Encino, a group of officials representing a major East Coast basketball tournament came by Coach Wooden's home. The officials met with Coach for a short time, then said they wanted to take him out to an expensive restaurant. "And because I was there," Puckett recalled, "they included me in the invitation."

Young Kim Puckett was excited at the prospect of going to a posh Los Angeles eatery, but Coach Wooden dashed his nephew's hopes and declined the invitation. After the delegation left, Coach turned to his young nephew and said, "Hey, I've got two free passes to Sizzler. Would you like to go?" Puckett recalled, "My uncle's eyes lit up, and he was as excited as I've ever seen him. A free meal at one of LA's finest restaurants held no appeal for him, but he couldn't imagine anything better than a steak and potato at Sizzler."

So Coach Wooden took his nephew to Sizzler. "Of all the times I've had with him," Puckett told me, "that was my favorite. It reminded me of my home and family in Indiana and all the simple pleasures that are part of being a Hoosier. My uncle had met presidents and movie stars and had coached the greatest basketball players of all time. Yet he was excited about a couple of free passes to Sizzler. It was the little things, the simple things, that always mattered to him most."

And it's the little things, the simple things, that should matter to you and me as well. When we break it all down, life is made up of little things, fundamental things, simple things. By focusing on the little things, we prepare ourselves to achieve our goals, to produce consistent high levels of performance and excellence, and to guard our character and build good habits.

Be attentive to the little things. Focus on doing a lot of little things well. Great achievements are the result of striving for perfection in all the seemingly minor details of life.

Little things make big things happen. They always have, and they always will.

Appendix 1

Additional Resources

IT WAS AN INCREDIBLE PRIVILEGE TO GET TO KNOW Coach John Wooden during the closing decade of his life. As you can tell from these pages, he left a deep imprint on me. Throughout each day, I have many opportunities to apply his life principles and maxims to real-life problems and situations. Every time I recall the conversations we had, I find myself wanting to be a better person, a better leader, a better Christian, a better influence on the people around me.

Even though it has been some time since he passed away, I still carry his wisdom with me. Even though I was never one of his players, but just an author who came into his life late in the game, I continually find myself wanting to please him, to make him proud of me.

Over the years, I've burrowed deep into his basketball insights, his life wisdom, and his unshakable faith. I've marveled at his humility and his generous spirit. I've been amazed at the way he answered every piece of mail, signed photos and copies of his Pyramid of Success, walked them down to the corner mailbox, and mailed them out at his own expense. He was a one-of-a-kind human being, a major celebrity who seemed completely unaware of his fame—or, at least, completely unfazed by it.

The saddest thing about Coach Wooden's passing is that young players, young coaches, and young businesspeople can no longer write to him, phone him, or visit him at his condo to draw from his wisdom. Yet we are fortunate to live in a media age, when so much of his wisdom is still available to us in books and recorded interviews.

So I encourage you to keep seeking out the wisdom of Coach John Wooden. I've written three books about his life and character: *How to Be like Coach Wooden*; *Coach Wooden: The Seven Principles That Shaped His Life and Will Change Yours*; and this book, *Coach Wooden's Greatest Secret*.

I would also recommend to you the following books by John Wooden with Steve Jamison: *The Essential Wooden: A Lifetime of Lessons on Leaders and Leadership*; *Wooden: A Lifetime of Observations and Reflections On and Off the Court*; *Wooden on Leadership: How to Create a Winning Organization*; *Coach Wooden's Leadership Game Plan for Success: 12 Lessons for Extraordinary Performance and Personal Excellence*; and *My Personal Best: Life Lessons from an All-American Journey*. Coach Wooden and Steve Jamison also produced a series of wonderful books for children, lavishly illustrated by Susan Cornelison: *Adventure Underground*; *Fiesta*; *Heroes of Beesville*; and *Inch and Miles: The Journey to Success*.

I would also recommend *Coach Wooden One-on-One: Inspiring Conversations on Purpose, Passion, and the Pursuit of Success* and *Coach Wooden's Pyramid of Success: Building Blocks for a Better Life*, both by John Wooden and Jay Carty. Another excellent book is *A Game Plan for Life: The Power of Mentoring* by Don Yaeger and John Wooden. *The John Wooden Pyramid of Success: The Authorized Biography* by Neville Johnson is packed with insights from Coach Wooden's life and philosophy. You should also read *They Call Me Coach* by John Wooden; *John Wooden's UCLA Offense* by John Wooden and Swen Nater; *Practical Modern Basketball* by John Wooden and Bill Walton; *You Haven't Taught until They Have Learned: John Wooden's Teaching Principles and Practices* by Swen Nater; and *Be Quick—but Don't Hurry! Finding Success in the Teachings of a Lifetime* by Andrew Hill and John Wooden.

I'll always be grateful that Coach Wooden lived to be ninety-nine years old, because he got to do a great deal of writing in the last decade of his life. Coach Wooden's last book was *The Wisdom of Wooden: My Century On and Off the Court* by John Wooden and Steve Jamison. It's a beautiful coffee table book that is truly a scrapbook of his life and career. He was actually sitting in his hospital bed, proofreading the galleys for that book, during the week he died.

Best of all, with just a few mouse clicks, you can actually see Coach John Wooden and hear him speak. You can hear his talk "The Difference between Winning and Succeeding" at TED.com. You can hear his multipart LeadershipTraQ interview on YouTube. You can find video from his memorial service and hear many of his former players talk about the life lessons they learned from him. And you can see many clips of Coach Wooden's Academy of Achievement interviews at Achievement.org.

If every human being on the planet lived by the principles that guided Coach John Wooden's life, we would eliminate 90 percent of the problems in this world. So I encourage you to seek out his wisdom. Immerse yourself in his values, his faith, and his insights for living a successful life. Soak up all you can, then share that wisdom with the people around you—with your friends and family members, your children and grandchildren, your teammates and co-workers, and strangers on the street. I can think of few more profitable ways to invest your time. I can think of few better ways to live your life.

Appendix 2

Little Things Build a Big Legacy

W HEN PEOPLE THINK OF THE TEAMS JOHN
Wooden coached, they often recall mega-talented
superstars such as Walt Hazzard, Kareem Abdul-
Jabbar, and Bill Walton. Some say, "Of course he won all those
championships. Look at the talent he had to work with." In fact,
some of Coach Wooden's best teams had no superstars at all.
They were simply teams made up of solid players with a dependable work ethic who listened to Coach's teaching and focused
on the little things. The players who applied Coach Wooden's
principles on the court usually went on to apply those same
principles in their lives after basketball. That's why so many
of Coach's Wooden's players went on to become champions in
life. Here are the rosters of Coach Wooden's ten greatest teams.

1963–64 UCLA Bruins Men's Basketball Team

The Bruins were led by senior guard Walt Hazzard, who has
been called the greatest playmaker in UCLA history. Hazzard

averaged 18.6 points per game and was honored as college basketball's player of the year. He was the number one pick in the NBA draft, enjoyed a ten-year NBA career, and was head coach at UCLA in the 1980s. Point guard Gail Goodrich led in scoring with an average of 21.5 points per game. Though the Bruins were not considered a title contender at the start of the season, they quickly earned the respect of fans, sportswriters, and opponents. In the NCAA championship game, Coach Wooden's Bruins defeated Duke 98–83, capping off a perfect 30–0 season.

#20 Mike Huggins	#42 Walt Hazzard
#24 Chuck Darrow	#44 Kenny Washington
#25 Gail Goodrich	#50 Jack Hirsch
#32 Doug McIntosh	#52 Rich Levin
#34 Vaughn Hoffman	#53 Keith Erickson
#35 Fred Slaughter	#54 Kim Stewart

1964–65 UCLA Bruins Men's Basketball Team

No one expected Coach Wooden's Bruins to have back-to-back championship seasons. Gail Goodrich and Keith Erickson were the only starters returning from the previous year's championship team. The 1964–65 season should have been a rebuilding year for the Bruins. Instead, they again captured the national championship, defeating Michigan 91–80 and finishing with a 28–2 record. Gail Goodrich set a school record in that game, scoring 42 points.

#20 John Lyons	#32 Doug McIntosh
#22 John Galbraith	#34 Vaughn Hoffman
#23 Kenny Washington	#35 Mike Lynn
#25 Gail Goodrich	#40 Freddie Goss

#43 Brice Chambers   #53 Keith Erickson
#52 Rich Levin   #54 Edgar Lacey

1966–67 UCLA Bruins Men's Basketball Team

Though the Bruins started four sophomores and a junior, they cut a wide swath through their opponents on the way to a 30–0 season and a third NCAA championship in four years. One of those sophomore starters was center Lew Alcindor—now known as Kareem Abdul-Jabbar—who set a new school scoring record of 56 points in his first varsity game (later topping himself with 61 points against Washington State). Alcindor averaged 29 points per game, and his trademark dunk shot made him so dominant that the league banned the dunk the following year. In 2008, ESPN named Alcindor "the greatest player in college basketball history." The Bruins defeated Dayton in the championship game 79–64.

#22 Kenny Heitz   #42 Lucius Allen
#24 Gene Sutherland   #44 Mike Warren
#25 Don Saffer   #45 Bill Sweek
#30 Neville Saner   #52 Dick Lynn
#33 Lew Alcindor   #53 Lynn Shackelford
#35 Jim Nielsen   #55 Joe Chrisman

1967–68 UCLA Bruins Men's Basketball Team

The entire starting lineup from the previous championship season was back, and the Bruins were favored to repeat—until a two-point loss to the Houston Cougars snapped a forty-seven-game winning streak, leaving UCLA ranked second in the nation. UCLA came roaring back in the NCAA semifinals, clobbering the Cougars 101–69. Lew Alcindor was named college player of the year.

#22 Kenny Heitz	#42 Lucius Allen
#25 Mike Lynn	#44 Mike Warren
#30 Neville Saner	#45 Bill Sweek
#33 Lew Alcindor	#53 Lynn Shackelford
#35 Jim Nielsen	#54 Edgar Lacey

1968–69 UCLA Bruins Men's Basketball Team

In game twenty-six of the season, the USC Trojans upset the Bruins 46–44—UCLA's first-ever loss at the school's home arena, Pauley Pavilion, built in 1965. The Bruins went on to win their third consecutive NCAA basketball title, defeating Coach Wooden's alma mater, Purdue, 92–72, for a season record of 29–1. Lew Alcindor averaged 24 points and 14.6 rebounds per game, finishing his UCLA career as the school's all-time scoring and rebounding leader.

#22 Kenny Heitz	#40 John Vallely
#30 Curtis Rowe	#42 Terry Schofield
#32 Steve Patterson	#45 Bill Sweek
#33 Lew Alcindor	#52 John Ecker
#34 George Farmer	#53 Lynn Shackelford
#35 Sidney Wicks	#54 Bill Seibert

1969–70 UCLA Bruins Men's Basketball Team

With the departure of Lew Alcindor to the NBA, pundits predicted the end of the Bruins dynasty. Only one of Coach Wooden's five starters, guard John Vallely, was a returning senior; three were juniors and one was a sophomore. Even without Alcindor, John Wooden's Bruins went 28–2, clinching their sixth NCAA championship in seven years with a win over Jacksonville. In that game, the Bruins overcame a nine-point halftime deficit to win 80–69.

#23 Kenny Booker	#35 Sidney Wicks
#24 Rick Betchley	#40 John Vallely
#25 Andy Hill	#42 Terry Schofield
#30 Curtis Rowe	#45 Henry Bibby
#32 Steve Patterson	#52 John Ecker
#34 Jon Chapman	#54 Bill Seibert

1970–71 UCLA Bruins Men's Basketball Team

Though the Bruins amassed an impressive season record of 29–1, it was a season of adversity. In seven games, Coach Wooden's players won by five points or less. Sidney Wicks gave UCLA the win against Oregon State with a final-second basket, and UCLA had to rally from a nine-point deficit in the final minutes of a game against USC. The Bruins came back from an eleven-point deficit against Cal State Long Beach in the NCAA regionals. Coach Wooden's Bruins defeated Villanova 68–62 for a seventh NCAA championship in eight years.

#23 Kenny Booker	#35 Sidney Wicks
#24 Rick Betchley	#43 Terry Schofield
#25 Andy Hill	#45 Henry Bibby
#30 Curtis Rowe	#52 John Ecker
#32 Steve Patterson	#53 Larry Hollyfield
#34 Jon Chapman	#54 Larry Farmer

1971–72 UCLA Bruins Men's Basketball Team

A perfect 30–0 record formed the foundation of UCLA's record eighty-eight-game winning streak. Led by sophomore center Bill Walton and sophomore forward Keith Wilkes, the Bruins dominated their opponents, winning games by an average margin of thirty points. UCLA clinched the NCAA championship with an 81–76 victory over Florida State—the eighth championship in nine years under Coach Wooden.

#22 Tommy Curtis	#43 Greg Lee
#25 Andy Hill	#45 Henry Bibby
#30 Vince Carson	#50 Gary Franklin
#31 Swen Nater	#52 Keith Wilkes
#32 Bill Walton	#53 Larry Hollyfield
#34 Jon Chapman	#54 Larry Farmer

1972–73 UCLA Bruins Men's Basketball Team

UCLA continued to dominate, winning all twenty-six regular-season games by six points or more while extending the longest winning streak in NCAA basketball history. The Bruins won their ninth championship in ten years under Coach Wooden by defeating the Memphis Tigers 87–66. Center Bill Walton stunned the crowd, making 21 of 22 field goal attempts and scoring 44 points—perhaps the greatest offensive performance in college basketball history.

#22 Tommy Curtis	#34 Dave Meyers
#25 Pete Trgovich	#35 Ralph Drollinger
#30 Vince Carson	#40 Casey Corliss
#31 Swen Nater	#42 Bob Webb
#32 Bill Walton	#43 Greg Lee

#50 Gary Franklin   #53 Larry Hollyfield

#52 Keith Wilkes   #54 Larry Farmer

1974–75 UCLA Bruins Men's Basketball Team

This was the last team John Wooden coached—and one of his all-time favorites. He especially loved these players because there were no superstars. Instead of relying on star power, they worked together as a team and focused on doing all the little things that would give them an extra edge over their opponents. The 1974–75 UCLA Bruins overcame adversity, finished the season with a 28-3 record, defeated the Kentucky Wildcats 92–85 in the NCAA title game, and sent Coach Wooden into retirement with his tenth championship in twelve years.

#22 Raymond Townsend   #44 Jim Spillane

#25 Pete Trgovich   #45 Andre McCarter

#31 Richard Washington   #50 Marvin Thomas

#32 Brett Vroman   #53 Wilbert Olinde

#34 Dave Meyers   #54 Marques Johnson

#35 Ralph Drollinger   #55 Gavin Smith

#40 Casey Corlisss

As ESPN's Rick Reilly observed, the humble and unassuming Coach John Wooden "never made more than $35,000 a year, including 1975, the year he won his tenth national championship, and never asked for a raise."[1]

Notes

Introduction: Little Things Make Big Things Happen

1. Kareem Abdul-Jabbar, "Appreciating the Wisdom of Wooden," *New York Times*, December 10, 2000, http://theater.nytimes.com/2000/12/10/sports/10JABB.html?pagewanted=all&_r=0.

2. Jon Robinson, "Dwyane Wade Interview, IGN.com, August 26, 2005, http://www.ign.com/articles/2005/08/26/dwyane-wade-interview-2?page=3.

3. ESPN, "Ryan Lochte Sets Meet Record," ESPN.com, May 13, 2012, http://m.espn.go.com/extra/olympics/story?storyId=7926518&lang=ES&wjb=.

4. Lancaster Adams, *Revelations of Your Self-Help Book Secrets: Neuroscience and Psychology of the Self-Help Literature* (Houston: Strategic, 2012), 94.

5. John Lloyd and John Mitchinson, *If Ignorance Is Bliss, Why Aren't There More Happy People?: Smart Quotes for Dumb Times* (New York: Crown, 2008), 313.

6. James Boswell, *The Life of Samuel Johnson, LL.D.* (London: Henry Baldwin, 1791), 235.

7. Frank Fitzpatrick, "Smith's Lament: Record, Record Go Away He Soon May Win His 877th Game. So Why Isn't He Happy?," *Philadelphia Inquirer*, March 13, 1997, http://articles.philly.com/1997-03-13/sports/25570906_1_ncaa-selection-committee-dean-smith-center-adolph-rupp.

8. John U. Bacon, *America's Corner Store: Walgreens' Prescription for Success* (Hoboken: Wiley, 2004), 98.

9. Alan Cohen, "It's the Little Things That Matter," *Fast Company*, January 18, 2008, http://www.fastcompany.com/627532/its-little-things-matter.

10. Robert I. Sutton, PhD, "Why 'Big Picture Only' Bosses Are the Worst," *Fast Company*, March 22, 2012, http://www.fastcompany.com/1825733/why-big-picture-only-bosses-are-worst.

11. "Value," D.U.O. Project, 1993, DoUntoOthers.org, http://www.dountoothers.org/money71706.html; Eastman School of Music, "Concerts and Events,"

2012–13 Concert Series, University of Rochester, http://www.esm.rochester.edu/concerts/.

Chapter 1: Little Things Are Fundamental to Achievement

1. John Wooden (as told to Devin Gordon), "First, How to Put On Your Socks," *Newsweek*, October 24, 1999, http://www.thedailybeast.com/newsweek/1999/10/24/first-how-to-put-on-your-socks.html.

2. John Wooden and Steve Jamison, *The Essential Wooden: A Lifetime of Lessons on Leaders and Leadership* (New York: McGraw-Hill, 2006), 72.

3. Jack Ramsay, "My Secrets to NBA Head Coaching Success," ESPN.com: NBA, September 19, 2002, http://sports.espn.go.com/nba/columns/story?columnist=ramsay_drjack&id=1434127.

4. Harvey B. Mackay, *Swim with the Sharks without Being Eaten Alive* (New York: HarperCollins, 2005), 135.

5. Whitey Herzog with Jonathan Pitts, *You're Missin' a Great Game: From Casey to Ozzie, the Magic of Baseball and How to Get It Back* (New York: Simon & Schuster, 1999), 27.

6. Yogi Berra with Dave Kaplan, *What Time Is It? You Mean Now?* (New York: Simon & Schuster, 2002), 70–71.

7. "Michael Jordan Bio," NBA Encyclopedia Playoff Edition, NBA.com, http://www.nba.com/history/players/jordan_bio.html.

8. Chip Lovitt, *Michael Jordan: Basketball's Best* (New York: Scholastic, 2002), 31.

9. Kristie Ackert and Roger Rubin, "Former Indianapolis Colts Coach Tony Dungy Addresses New York Yankees before Loss to Red Sox," *New York Daily News*, September 26, 2010, http://www.nydailynews.com/sports/baseball/yankees/indianapolis-colts-coach-tony-dungy-addresses-new-york-yankees-loss-red-sox-article-1.444157.

10. Mitch Meyerson with Mary Eule Scarborough, *Mastering Online Marketing* (Irvine, CA: Entrepreneur Media, 2008), 237.

11. John Ashcroft, *Lessons from a Father to His Son* (Nashville: Thomas Nelson, 1998), Kindle edition, unnumbered pages.

12. Ibid.

13. Robert I. Sutton, "Good Bosses Are the Same Today as They Were in 1992," *Fast Company*, March 16, 2012, http://www.fastcompany.com/1825035/good-bosses-are-same-today-they-were-1992.

14. Carter Malkasian, *The Korean War* (New York: Rosen, 2009), 36; Bong Lee, *The Unfinished War: Korea* (New York: Algora, 2003), 111; Stephen P. Rosen, *Winning the Next War* (Ithaca, NY: Cornell University Press, 1991), 33.

15. Steve Turley, "Book Review: *You Haven't Taught until They Have Learned: John Wooden's Teaching Principles and Practices* by Swen Nater & Ronald Gillimore," *Issues in Teacher Education*, Spring 2008, 105, http://www1.chapman.edu/ITE/14turleyreview.pdf.

16. Alexander Wolff, "16 John Wooden," *Sports Illustrated*, September 19, 1994, http://sportsillustrated.cnn.com/vault/article/magazine/MAG1005681/.

17. Wooden and Jamison, *Essential Wooden*, 65.

18. John R. Wooden with Swen Nater, *UCLA Offensive* (Champaign, IL: Human Kinetics, 2006), 31.

19. John Wooden with Steve Jamison, *Wooden on Leadership: How to Create a Winning Organization* (New York: McGraw-Hill, 2005), 99.

Chapter 2: Little Things Lead to Simplicity—and Success

1. Neville L. Johnson, *The John Wooden Pyramid of Success* (Los Angeles: Cool Titles, 2003), 448.

2. Billy Packer with Roland Lazenby, *Why We Win* (New York: Masters Press, 1999), 45.

3. Johnson, *John Wooden Pyramid of Success*, 419.

4. James M. McPherson, *This Mighty Scourge: Perspectives on the Civil War* (New York: Oxford University Press, 2007), 112.

5. Ulysses Simpson Grant, statement to John Hill Brinton at the start of his Tennessee River Campaign, early 1862, as quoted in John Hill Brinton, *Personal Memoirs of John H. Brinton, Major and Surgeon U.S.V., 1861–1865* (1914), 239.

6. Alan Axelrod, *Eisenhower on Leadership: Ike's Enduring Lessons in Total Victory Management* (San Francisco: Jossey-Bass, 2006), 100.

7. Brian Tracy, *Victory!: Applying the Proven Principles of Military Strategy to Achieve Greater Success in Your Business and Personal Life* (New York: AMA-COM, 2002), 167.

8. David H. Freedman, *Corps Business: The 30 Management Principles of the U.S. Marines* (New York: HarperCollins, 2000), 10.

9. Ibid.

10. Arthur P. Brill Jr., "One Certainty for Marine Corps: Constant Change," Navy league of the United States, November 2003, http://www.navyleague.org/sea_power/nov_03_28.php.

11. Oren Harari, *The Leadership Secrets of Colin Powell* (New York: McGraw-Hill, 2003), 260.

12. Vince Lombardi Jr., *The Essential Vince Lombardi: Words and Wisdom to Motivate, Inspire, and Win* (New York: McGraw-Hill, 2002), 164.

13. Vince Lombardi Jr., *What It Takes to Be #1: Vince Lombardi on Leadership* (New York: McGraw-Hill, 2001), 42.

14. Stephen R. Fox, *Big Leagues: Professional Baseball, Football, and Basketball in National Memory* (Lincoln: University of Nebraska Press/Bison Books, 1998), 388.

15. John C. Maxwell, *Leadership Gold: Lessons I've Learned from a Lifetime of Leading* (Nashville: Thomas Nelson, 2008), 102.

16. Hans Hofmann, "Hans Hofmann: Quotes," HansHofmann.net, http://www.hanshofmann.net/quotes.html#.UV8s1sqRc9Y.

17. Joshua Fost, *If Not God, Then What?* (Portland, OR: Clearhead Studios, 2007), 93.

18. Kevin G. Hall, "Before Bombings, Feds Questioned Massachusetts Security Plan," McClatchy Newspapers, April 16, 2013, http://www.mcclatchydc.com/2013/04/16/188726/before-bombings-feds-questioned.html.

19. Sheila Murray Bethel, *A New Breed of Here: Eight Leadership Qualities That Matter Most in the Real World* (New York: Penguin, 2009), 161.

20. Carmine Gallo, "The Three Communication Skills That Make Suze Orman an Influential Celebrity," *Forbes*, March 20, 2013, http://www.forbes.com/sites/carminegallo/2013/03/20/three-communication-skills-that-make-suze-orman-an-influential-celebrity/.

21. Robert Slater, *Twenty-Nine Leadership Secrets from Jack Welch* (New York: McGraw-Hill Professional, 2003), 15.

22. Robert Slater, *Jack Welch and the GE Way: Management Insights and Leadership Secrets of the Legendary CEO* (New York: McGraw-Hill, 2001), 139.

23. Alex Law, "Car of the Century," *Auto123*, December 22, 1999, http://www.auto123.com/en/news/car-of-the-century?artid=1082.

24. Jim Rasenberger, *America, 1908: The Dawn of Flight, the Race to the Pole, the Invention of the Model T, and the Making of a Modern America* (New York: Scribner, 2007), 222.

25. John Wooden with Steve Jamison, *Wooden's Complete Guide to Leadership* (New York: McGraw-Hill, 2011), 197–98.

26. Michael Mink, "John Wooden Aimed for Excellence and Scored Big," *Investor's Business Daily*, June 10, 2010, http://news.investors.com/management-leaders-in-success/061010-536929-john-wooden-aimed-for-excellence-and-scored-big.htm?p=full.

Chapter 3: Little Things Prepare You for Great Things

1. John Wooden with Jack Tobin, *They Call Me Coach* (New York: McGraw-Hill, 2004), 218.

2. Ibid.

3. Michael Mink, "John Wooden Won 10 Titles by Putting Process First," *Investor's Business Daily*, April 5, 2013, http://news.investors.com/management-leaders-in-success/040513-650815-john-wooden-won-by-putting-process-first.htm?ven=rss.

4. Og Mandino, *Og Mandino's University of Success* (New York: Bantam, 1982), 43–44.

5. Larry Chang, *Wisdom for the Soul: Five Millennia of Prescriptions for Spiritual Healing* (Washington, DC: Gnosophia, 2006), 283.

6. Creed King, *Don't Play for the Tie: Bear Bryant on Life* (Nashville: Rutledge Hill, 2006), 100.

7. Curt Schleier, "Don Shula Dived into Details and Made a Miami Splash," *Investor's Business Daily*, October 8, 2012, http://news.investors.com/management-leaders-in-success/100812-628489-dolphins-appreciate-shulas-attention-to-detail.htm?p=full.

8. Ibid.

9. Ibid.

10. Ibid.

11. Ally Rogers, "Slugger Museum 125 Years of History," *Gold Standard*, June 17, 2009, http://www.fkgoldstandard.com/content/slugger-museum-125-years-history?quicktabs_2=1.

12. David Cataneo, *I Remember Ted Williams: Anecdotes and Memories of Baseball's Splendid Splinter* (Nashville: Cumberland House, 2002), 30.

13. Ibid., 36–37.

14. John Wooden with Steve Jamison, *Wooden: A Lifetime of Observations and Reflections On and Off the Court* (Chicago: Contemporary Books, 1997), 75–76.

Chapter 4: Little Things Are the Key to Achieving Your Goals

1. Neville L. Johnson, *The John Wooden Pyramid of Success* (Los Angeles: Cool Titles, 2003), 419.

2. John Wooden, "John Wooden Interview: Basketball's Coaching Legend," Academy of Achievement, interview conducted February 27, 1996, posted March 3, 2010, http://www.achievement.org/autodoc/page/woo0int-1.

3. John Wooden with Steve Jamison, *Wooden on Leadership: How to Create a Winning Organization* (New York: McGraw-Hill, 2005), 135–36.

4. Brandi L. Bates, "Quotable Quote," GoodReads.com, http://www.goodreads.com/quotes/570213-do-little-things-every-day-that-no-one-else-seems.

5. Carter Henderson, "World-Scale Entrepreneuring," *The Rotarian*, April 1988, 23.

6. David J. Schwartz, *The Magic of Thinking Big* (New York: Simon & Schuster, 1959, 1987), 265.

7. Ibid.

8. Patrick Morley, *The Man in the Mirror: Solving the 24 Problems Men Face* (Grand Rapids: Zondervan, 2011), 204.

9. Nobel Women's Initiative, "Meet the Laureates: Wangari Maathai—Kenya 2004, Founding Member," NobelWomensInitiative.org, http://nobelwomensinitiative.org/meet-the-laureates/wangari-maathai/.

10. Madan Birla, *FedEx Delivers: How the World's Leading Shipping Company Keeps Innovating and Outperforming the Competition* (Hoboken: Wiley, 2005), 90–91.

11. Brian Thomsen, *The Awful Truths* (New York: HarperCollins, 2006), 153.

12. Jim Calhoun with Richard Ernsberger Jr., *A Passion to Lead: Seven Leadership Secrets for Success in Business, Sports, and Life* (New York: St. Martin's, 2007), 27.

13. Amy Boothe Green and Howard E. Green, *Remembering Walt: Favorite Memories of Walt Disney* (New York: Hyperion, 1999), 163.

14. Told to the author by Disney associate Bob Gurr in a telephone interview.

15. Told to the author by Disney historian Paul Anderson of Brigham Young University in a telephone interview.

16. John Rosevear, "6 Annoying Ways to Build Wealth," *Motley Fool*, November 27, 2007, http://www.fool.com/personal-finance/general/2007/11/27/6-annoying-ways-to-build-wealth.aspx.

17. John Simpson and Jennifer Speake, *A Dictionary of Proverbs* (New York: Oxford, 2008), 187.

18. S. L. Parker, "Nightingale-Conant Presents S. L. Parker: 212°: The Extra Degree," Nightingale.com, http://www.nightingale.com/ae_article.aspx?a=212_theextradegree&i=236.

19. Ibid.

20. Dru Scott Decker, *Finding More Time in Your Life* (Eugene, OR: Harvest House, 2001), 47–49.

21. Zig Ziglar, *Courtship after Marriage: Romance Can Last a Lifetime* (Nashville: Thomas Nelson, 1990), 93.

22. Andrew Hill with John Wooden, *Be Quick—but Don't Hurry!: Finding Success in the Teachings of a Lifetime* (New York: Simon & Schuster, 2001), 77–78.

Chapter 5: Little Things Produce Consistency

1. André McCarter, "The Pyramid of Success," *Guideposts*, http://www.guideposts.org/inspirational-stories/inspiring-stories-ucla-coach-john-wooden.

2. John Wooden with Steve Jamison, *Wooden on Leadership: How to Create a Winning Organization* (New York: McGraw-Hill, 2005), 109.

3. Tony Dungy with Nathan Whitaker, "An Unforgettable Season," Beliefnet.com, August 2007, http://www.beliefnet.com/Entertainment/Books/2007/08/An-Unforgettable-Season.aspx?p=2.

4. Truett Cathy, *Eat Mor Chikin: Inspire More People* (Decatur, GA: Looking Glass Books, 2002), 68–69.

5. Paul Buyer, *Working toward Excellence: 8 Values for Achieving Uncommon Success in Work and Life* (New York: Morgan James, 2012), xxii.

6. Ruth Graham, *A Legacy of Faith: Things I Learned from My Father* (Grand Rapids: Zondervan, 2009), Kindle edition, unnumbered pages.

7. Robert Slater, *Jack Welch and the GE Way: Management Insights and Leadership* (New York: McGraw-Hill, 2001), 54–55.

8. Bob Sutton, "Polly LaBarre On 'Jargon Monoxide,'" Work Matters, March 3, 2007, http://bobsutton.typepad.com/my_weblog/2007/03/polly_labarre_t.html.

9. Alex Keegan, "Dealing with Rejection," *Writers Write: The Internet Writing Journal*, October 1998, http://www.writerswrite.com/journal/oct98/keegan12.htm.

10. McCarter, "Pyramid of Success."

Chapter 6: Little Things Lead to Excellence

1. Neville L. Johnson, *The John Wooden Pyramid of Success* (Los Angeles: Cool Titles, 2003), 86.

2. Ibid.

3. Ibid., 87.

4. John Wooden with Steve Jamison, *Wooden: A Lifetime of Observations and Reflections On and Off the Court* (Chicago: Contemporary Books, 1997), 200.

5. Julie M. Fenster, *In the Words of Great Business Leaders* (New York: Wiley, 2000), 149–50.

6. John D. Rockefeller, *Random Reminiscences of Men and Events* (New York: Doubleday, Page & Co., 1909), 21, http://www.gutenberg.org/files/17090/17090-h/17090-h.htm.

7. Lucy McCauley, "How May I Help You?," *Fast Company*, March 2000, http://www.fastcompany.com/38973/how-may-i-help-you.

8. Ibid.

9. Lisa Earle McLeod, "The One-Minute Change That Will Transform Your Company," *Fast Company*, December 3, 2012, http://www.fastcompany.com/3003455/one-minute-change-will-transform-your-company.

10. Harriet Beecher Stowe, "The Cathedral," *The Writings of Harriet Beecher Stowe*, vol. 8 (Boston & New York: Houghton-Mifflin, 1896), 414.

11. Susan Corso, "Back in Lady Liberty's Head," *Huffington Post*, July 6, 2009, http://www.huffingtonpost.com/dr-susan-corso/back-in-lady-libertys-hea_b_225915.html.

12. Joseph Michelli, *The New Gold Standard: 5 Leadership Principles for Creating a Legendary Customer Experience Courtesy of the Ritz-Carlton Hotel Company* (New York: McGraw-Hill Professional, 2008), 112–13.

13. Ibid., 113–14.

14. Shawn Graham, "Careers: Great Bosses and the Power of Silly Putty," *Fast Company*, October 8, 2007, http://www.fastcompany.com/660989/careers-great-bosses-and-power-silly-putty.

15. Ibid.

16. Don Soderquist, *Live, Learn, Lead to Make a Difference* (Nashville: J. Countryman, 2006), 29–31.

17. Joe D. Batten and Mark Victor Hansen, *The Master Motivator: Secrets of Inspiring Leadership* (Deerfield Beach, FL: Health Communications, Inc., 1995), 77.

18. Fellowship of Christian Athletes, *The Greatest Coach Ever: Timeless Wisdom and Insights of John Wooden* (Ventura, CA: Regal Books, 2010), 85.

19. John Wooden with Steve Jamison, *Wooden on Leadership: How to Create a Winning Organization* (New York: McGraw-Hill, 2005), 144.

20. Ibid., 143.

21. Ibid., 146.

Chapter 7: Little Things Guard Your Character

1. John Wooden with Jack Tobin, *They Call Me Coach* (New York: McGraw-Hill, 2004), 26.

2. John Wooden and Steve Jamison, *The Essential Wooden: A Lifetime of Lessons on Leaders and Leadership* (New York: McGraw-Hill, 2006), 179.

3. Rick Warren, "God Uses Little Things to Test Your Integrity," PurposeDriven.com, April 23, 2013, http://purposedriven.com/blogs/dailyhope/the-little-things-count-/.

4. Zig Ziglar, "Favorite Quotations," Daily Celebrations, http://www.dailycelebrations.com/zig2.htm.

5. C. S. Lewis, *The Complete C. S. Lewis Signature Classics* (New York: HarperOne, 2007), 220.

6. C. S. Lewis, *Mere Christianity*, Book 3, Christian Behaviour, Chap. 9: Charity, http://www.pbs.org/wgbh/questionofgod/ownwords/mere2.html.

7. Ibid.

8. Dave Egner, "'Little' Sin," FirstImpressions, Wilmington First Assembly of God, November 14, 2003, http://www.wfa.org/newsletter/archive/2003/0346_031114/0346_031114.html.

9. John Wooden with Steve Jamison, *Wooden: A Lifetime of Observations and Reflections On and Off the Court* (Chicago: Contemporary Books, 1997), 197–99.

10. Dennis J. De Haan, "All The Dead Will Rise!," *Our Daily Bread*, March 31, 2002, http://odb.org/2002/03/31/all-the-dead-will-rise/.

11. Jaroldeen Edwards, *Celebration!*, Beloveddaughter.Wordpress.com, March 5, 2008, http://beloveddaughter.wordpress.com/2008/03/05/the-daffodil-principle-taken-from-celebration-by-jaroldeen-edwards/.

12. Pat Williams, *Coach Wooden: The 7 Principles That Shaped His Life and Will Change Yours* (Grand Rapids: Revell, 2011), 26–27.

13. John Wooden with Steve Jamison, *Wooden: A Lifetime of Observations and Reflections On and Off the Court* (Chicago: Contemporary Books, 1997), 6–7.

14. UCLA Athletics, "UCLA's Legendary Former Basketball Coach John Wooden Passes Away," UCLABruins.com, June 4, 2010, http://www.uclabruins.com/ViewArticle.dbml?DB_OEM_ID=30500&ATCLID=207904616.

15. Wooden, *Wooden*, 170.

16. Ibid., 28.

17. Ibid., 42.

Chapter 8: Little Things Yield a Habit of Success

1. Colin Powell with Joseph E. Persico, *My American Journey* (New York: Random House, 1996), 198.

2. Joel Weldon, video of speech titled "Elephants Don't Bite!," uploaded November 12, 2009, http://www.youtube.com/watch?v=PXsCjgjeucI.

3. Tryon Edwards, *A Dictionary of Thoughts: Being a Cyclopedia of Laconic Quotations* (Detroit: F. B. Dickerson Co., 1908), 212.

4. Ibid.

5. Og Mandino, *The Greatest Secret in the World* (New York: Bantam, 1972), 11.

6. John Maxwell, *Put Your Dream to the Test: 10 Questions That Will Help You See It and Seize It* (Nashville: Thomas Nelson, 2011), 61.

7. Elbert Hubbard, *Little Journeys to the Homes of Great Business Men: John Jacob Astor* (East Aurora, NY: Roycroft, 1909), http://www.gutenberg.org/files/412/old/jastr10.txt.

8. Brian Tracy, *Something for Nothing: The All-Consuming Desire That Turns the American Dream into a Social Nightmare* (Nashville: Thomas Nelson, 2005), 73.

9. Ed Gary George, *Winning Is a Habit: Vince Lombardi on Winning, Success, and the Pursuit of Excellence* (New York: HarperCollins, 1997), 2.

10. Harry Allen Smith, *The Life and Legend of Gene Fowler* (New York: Morrow, 1977), 299.

11. Hal Urban, *Life's Greatest Lessons: 20 Things That Matter* (New York: Simon & Schuster, 2003), 67.

12. Avery Johnson with Roy S. Johnson, *Aspire Higher* (New York: HarperCollins, 2009), 192–93.

13. Og Mandino, *Og Mandino's University of Success* (New York: Bantam, 1982), 191.

14. Brian Tracy, *Million Dollar Habits* (Irvine, CA: Entrepreneur Press, 2006), 90.

15. Ibid.

16. Ronald Reagan, Commencement Address, "Keepers of the Peace," McAlister Field House, the Citadel, the Military College of South Carolina, May 15, 1993, http://www3.citadel.edu/pao/addresses/reagan.htm.

17. Neville L. Johnson, *The John Wooden Pyramid of Success: The Authorized Biography* (Los Angeles: Cool Titles, 2003), 122–23.

18. John Wooden with Steve Jamison, *Wooden on Leadership: How to Create a Winning Organization* (New York: McGraw-Hill, 2005), 72.

Appendix 2: Little Things Build a Big Legacy

1. Rick Reilly, "Life of Reilly: One Coach Still Knows More Than All the Others Combined, and He's Been Retired for Three Decades," *ESPN: The Magazine*, October 28, 2008, http://sports.espn.go.com/espnmag/story?id=3669154.

CONNECT WITH PAT

We would love to hear from you. Please send your comments about this book to Pat Williams:

pwilliams@orlandomagic.com

Pat Williams
c/o Orlando Magic
8701 Maitland Summit Boulevard
Orlando, FL 32810

If you would like to set up a speaking engagement for Pat, please contact his assistant, Andrew Herdliska:
(407) 916-2401
aherdliska@orlandomagic.com

PATWILLIAMS.COM

  OrlandoMagicPat

Everyone has INFLUENCE.
What will you do with the INFLUENCE you have?

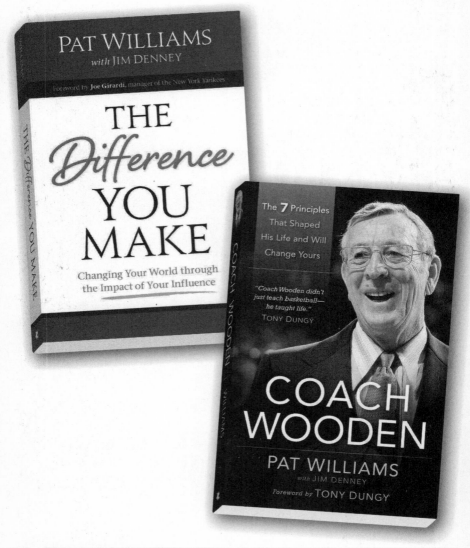